MATERNAL ATTACHMENT
and
MOTHERING DISORDERS

Summary Publications in the Johnson & Johnson Baby Products Company Pediatric Round Table Series:

1. *Maternal Attachment and Mothering Disorders:*
   A Round Table
   Edited by Marshall H. Klaus, M.D.,
          Treville Leger and
          Mary Anne Trause, Ph.D.

2. *Social Responsiveness of Infants*
   Edited by Evelyn B. Thoman, Ph.D.
          and Sharland Trotter

3. *Learning Through Play*
   By Paul Chance, Ph.D.

4. *The Communication Game*
   Edited by Abigail Peterson Reilly, Ph.D.

5. *Infants At Risk: Assessment and Intervention*
   Edited by Catherine Caldwell Brown

6. *Birth, Interaction and Attachment*
   Edited by Marshall H. Klaus, M.D.
          and Martha Oschrin Robertson

MATERNAL ATTACHMENT
and
MOTHERING DISORDERS

Edited by
Marshall H. Klaus, M.D.
Treville Leger
and
Mary Anne Trause, Ph.D.

Second Edition
1982

Sponsored by

Johnson & Johnson

BABY PRODUCTS COMPANY

Library of Congress Cataloging in Publication Data
Main entry under title:

Maternal Attachment and Mothering Disorders:
  A Round Table

  (Johnson & Johnson Baby Products Company pediatric
round table series; 1)

Proceedings of the Round Table on Maternal Attachment and
Mothering Disorders, held in Sausalito, Calif., Oct. 18-19, 1974.

Bibliography: p.
  1. Infants (Newborn) — Family relationships — Congresses.
2. Mother and child — Congresses. I. Klaus, Marshall H.
II. Leger, Treville. III. Trause, Mary Anne. IV. Johnson &
Johnson Baby Products Company. V. Round Table on
Maternal Attachment and Mothering Disorders (1974:
Sausalito, Calif.) IV. Series. (DNLM: 1. Mother-child
relations — Congresses. 2. Maternal behavior — Congresses.
WS 105.5.F2 M424 1982)
RF255.M34 1982 618.92'01'019 82-13048

ISBN 0-931562-04-X

Printed in the United States of America

*To Child Health Care Professionals
and Parents of this and future generations
who will be beneficiaries of greater knowledge
of maternal attachment*

Contents

Participants

THOMAS F. ANDERS, M.D.
Professor of Child Psychiatry
Department of Psychiatry
Stanford University Medical School
Stanford, California

SUZANNE ARMS
Author
Mill Valley, California

GIULIO J. BARBERO, M.D.
Professor and Chairman,
Department of Child Health
University of Missouri Medical Center
Columbia, Missouri

KATHRYN BARNARD, Ph.D.
Professor of Nursing
University of Washington
Seattle, Washington

WILLIAM BORTREE
Group Product Director
Johnson & Johnson Baby Products Co.
Piscataway, New Jersey

T. BERRY BRAZELTON, M.D.
Associate Professor of Pediatrics
Harvard University
Cambridge, Massachusetts

DAVID CREWS, Ph.D.
Post-doctoral Fellow
University of California
Berkeley, California

ALISON FLEMING, Ph.D.
Post-doctoral Fellow
University of California
Berkeley, California

SELMA FRAIBERG, M.S.W.
Professor of Child Psychoanalysis
    and Director/Child Development Project
University of Michigan
Ann Arbor, Michigan

ROSAMUND GARDNER, Ph.D.
Chief Psychologist and Co-Director
Mother-Infant Research Project
Childrens Hospital Medical Center
Oakland, California

ROSE GROBSTEIN, M.S.W.
Chief Pediatric Social Worker
  and Research Associate
Stanford University Medical Center
Stanford, California

RAY HELFER, M.D.
Professor of Human Development
Michigan State University
East Lansing, Michigan

CONSTANCE KEEFER, M.D.
Fellow in Child Development
Children's Hospital Medical Center
Boston, Massachusetts

JOHN H. KENNELL, M.D.
Professor of Pediatrics
Case Western Reserve University
Cleveland, Ohio

MARSHALL H. KLAUS, M.D.
Professor of Pediatrics
Case Western Reserve University
Cleveland, Ohio

ANNELIESE KORNER, Ph.D.
Senior Scientist
Department of Psychiatry
Stanford University Medical School
Stanford, California

RAVEN LANG
Lay Midwife
Lantzville, Vancouver Island
Canada

P. HERBERT LEIDERMAN, M.D.
Professor of Psychiatry
Stanford University Medical Center
Stanford, California

NANCY MILLS
Lay Midwife
Sonoma, California

LAWRENCE MORIN, Ph.D.
Post-doctoral Fellow
University of California
Berkeley, California

ROSS D. PARKE, Ph.D.
Fels Clinical Professor of
  Pediatric Research
University of Cincinnati
  College of Medicine
Cincinnati, Ohio

E. J. QUILLIGAN, M.D.
Professor and Chairman
Department of Obstetrics and
  Gynecology
University of Southern California
  School of Medicine
Womens Hospital
Los Angeles, California

R. B. ROCK, JR.
Director of Professional Relations
Johnson & Johnson
  Domestic Operating Company
New Brunswick, New Jersey

JAY S. ROSENBLATT, Ph.D.
Director, Institute of Animal Behavior
Rutgers University
Newark, New Jersey

STEVEN SAWCHUK, M.D.
Director of Medical Services
Johnson & Johnson Baby Products Co.
Piscataway, New Jersey

BRUCE SEMPLE, M.D.
Director, Medical and
  Regulatory Affairs
Johnson & Johnson Research
North Brunswick, New Jersey

DANIEL N. STERN, M.D.
Chief, Department of Developmental
  Processes
New York State Psychiatric Institute
  and Columbia University
New York, New York

MARY ANNE TRAUSE, Ph.D.
Research Associate
Department of Pediatrics
Case Western Reserve University
  Medical School
Cleveland, Ohio

Preface

The Preface to a second edition (even though changes are largely in format) is an appropriate place to comment on events which led up to the revision. In the early seventies the Johnson & Johnson Baby Products Company embarked on a program which sought to share with child health care professionals new information at the innovative edge of pediatric health and development. As a major element in this thrust, the company initiated a series of Pediatric Round Tables, of which *Maternal Attachment and Mothering Disorders* was the first. We were fortunate to have Marshall H. Klaus, M.D. as moderator and to have as participants some of the foremost medical and social scientists in the world. Although they all know each other from their writings, it was the first time they met together — and their discussion was truly charged with excitement.

The result of these discussions was this summary publication on *Maternal Attachment* and, as sponsors, the Johnson & Johnson Baby Products Company was truly interested in sharing its information. In the seven years since its publication, *Maternal Attachment* has gone through seven printings, with over 110,000 copies in circulation. It is particularly gratifying to know that well over half of these books have been used in teaching situations, both by child health care professionals and the lay public. And, in redesigning this publication to conform with others in the Johnson & Johnson Pediatric Round Table Series, the company hopes to make its contents more readily identifiable and appealing to those in the field of child health and development who have yet to discover it.

Robert B. Rock, Jr., M.A., M.P.A.
Director, Professional Relations

Introduction

Marshall H. Klaus, M.D.

During the past 40 years, Bowlby and Spitz have elaborated in great detail the process by which the human infant becomes attached to its mother. The Round Table on *Maternal Attachment and Mothering Disorders* is about the process of attachment in the opposite direction, from parent to infant. This specific field has become an important and significant area of pediatrics. Therefore, the Johnson & Johnson Baby Products Company initiated a Round Table on *Maternal Attachment and Mothering Disorders.*

The interest in studying the parent-to-infant bond was, in part, stimulated 10-15 years ago by the personnel of intensive care nurseries who observed that after heroic measures had been used to save small premature or sick infants, some would soon return to the hospital battered by their parents. The question arose as to what went wrong.

The purpose of this Round Table was to bring together clinicians and researchers from different disciplines who are presently studying the development of this attachment in parents of normal infants, parents of premature or sick infants, parents of battered or failure-to-thrive infants, as well as students of the attachment process in various animal species. Thus, the conference brought together psychologists, psychoanalysts, child psychiatrists, pediatricians, social workers, midwives, nurses, an obstetrician, and an animal behaviorist. To share the exciting data, thoughts, and perceptions of this group with a larger audience, the editors have summarized each presentation and included the especially stimulating or provocative parts of the discussion.

The Round Table consisted of three segments: (1) *"Disorders of Attachment"* featured the problems of failure-to-thrive, child abuse and neglect as they affected infants and their parents, focusing on the disruptive mechanisms, which result in these abnormalities. (2) *"The Process of Attachment"* in which some interesting parallels in behavior patterns of humans and animals were reviewed, and parent-child interaction as a developmental force was discussed. The role of the father was presented, and it was emphasized that the father can play a very useful role by interacting with the infant and the mother. (3) *"Problems of Attachment"* stressed the various parent visiting practices prevalent in intensive care nurseries in the United States. It was emphasized that mothers of premature infants should be permitted to have early physical contact with their infants in order to establish early mother-infant bonding.

This new and exciting area has proven to have long-range effects on not only the infant but also the parents. The participants of the round table stressed the many factors which can influence this very important time period in the life of the family and the simple but practical aspects of care, which can easily be implemented to help prevent the development of these conditions.

We especially thank Mr. Robert B. Rock, Jr., Dr. Steven Sawchuk, and the Johnson & Johnson Baby Products Company for their help in supporting this meeting and solving the innumerable tasks involved in its planning.

PART ONE
DISORDERS
OF
ATTACHMENT

Failure-to-Thrive
by Giulio Barbero, M.D.

The conference began with Dr. Barbero's presentation of two major problems, the failure-to-thrive (FTT) infant and the battered child. His study of these disturbances in maternal behavior began twenty-six years ago, when during his residency, he was presented with an emaciated and debilitated child, with no diagnosable organic etiology. Soon after being admitted, the boy developed a voracious appetite and rapidly gained weight. Upon being released from the hospital, the boy pleaded, "Please don't send me home." "However," Dr. Barbero reminisced, "he was released and taken home. A week or so later, he was re-admitted, and died within sixteen hours. The experience changed my outlook as a physician; I couldn't understand what had happened." Dr. Barbero described his further investigations which revealed that such unexplained failure-to-thrive was a frequent phenomenon at many hospitals.

Beginning by categorizing failure-to-thrive children as those who fell below the third weight percentile without known organic etiology, Dr. Barbero and his colleagues directed their initial efforts toward establishing diagnostic criteria. Study of infants with this problem led to the following clinical criteria:

1. Weight below the third percentile with subsequent weight gain in the presence of appropriate nurturing.
2. No evidence of systemic disease or abnormality on physical examination and laboratory investigation which explained growth failure.
3. Developmental retardation with subsequent acceleration of development following appropriate stimulation and feeding.
4. Clinical signs of deprivation which decrease in a more nurturing environment.
5. Presence of significant environmental psychosocial disruption.

Dr. Barbero pointed out that five percent of pediatric admissions in his hospital were below the third percentile in weight, and that a significant number of this five percent met all five diagnostic criteria.

He then cited the fifth criterion as central to this conference, and rephrased it in the question, "What is significant in terms of environmental psychosocial disruption?"

Returning to the clinical observations of failure-to-thrive, he began by talking about the eyes, a theme that at times seemed to be central to the conference. In sharp contrast to normal infants (e.g., as described by Drs. Brazelton and Stern), Dr. Barbero found failure-to-thrive infants to be characterized by numerous bizarre eye behaviors. These infants display a wide-eyed gaze, and tend to continually scan their environment and, may at times, avoid eye-to-eye contact. This avoidance occurs in various forms, ranging from simply looking away to actively covering the face and eyes with a hand or turning away from caregivers to face the wall.

Neurologically, Dr. Barbero described FTT's as centering around two extremes, the spastic and rigid babies on one end and the "floppy" babies, i.e., those with an extreme decrease in muscle tone "who practically fall through your hands" at the other. Regardless of which extreme they represent, the FTT's tended to be almost immobile.

As with his first failure-to-thrive twenty-six years earlier, Dr. Barbero observed improvement in FTT's during their hospitalization. He described an especially striking finding that social and behavioral development (e.g., establishment of normal eye contact) invariably preceded physical and neurological improvement. In conjunction with this startling observation, he believes that a frequent error in pediatrics is to automatically attribute failure-to-thrive to a known or suspected systemic disorder, while ignoring psychosocial factors. He presented a particularly impressive example of a child with chronic diarrhea and inability to absorb food. When moved into the hospital environment, his condition soon became normal, with very little medical intervention. Dr. Barbero related similar cases including an even more severe FTT who was initially believed to suffer from cerebral palsy but who, within a few months in his new hospital environment, showed development which clearly contradicted the initial diagnosis. "It is all too easy for us as pediatricians to apply labels to individuals and to begin extensive kinds of therapy when, perhaps, the therapy should be of a different sort."

Then, focusing on the issue of psychosocial disruption, he reviewed a number of representative experiences and observations that led him to investigate this area. Having examined a failure-to-thrive baby in extreme condition, he spoke with the mother and asked her the routine question, "What happened?" The mother responded with the apparent non sequitur, "My husband went away." Dr. Barbero, grappling with this apparent anomaly realized with further questioning that the mother was emotionally traumatized by a life history of repeated abandonment, which had severely affected her mothering ability.

Such experiences prompted Dr. Barbero's systematic study of disturbing events that may explain disorders in maternal attachment. Figure 1 illustrates events in the life history of the families which Dr. Barbero found to be significant.

1. DISORDERS IN MATERNAL ATTACHMENT
   — PAST EVENTS
   A. Early Parental Life Deprivations
   B. Loss of Parent Figures Early in the
      Life of the Parent
   C. Illness During Parent's Childhood
   D. Death or Illness in Prior Children

2. DISORDERS IN MATERNAL ATTACHMENT
   — PREGNANCY EVENTS
   A. Protracted Emotional or Physical Illness

B. Deaths or Major Illness of Key Family Figures
3. DISORDERS IN MATERNAL ATTACHMENT
   — PERINATAL EVENTS
   A. Complication of Parturition
   B. Acute Illness in Mother or Infant
   C. Prematurity
   D. Congenital Defects
   E. Diseases
   F. Iatrogenic or Institutional Disruptions

4. DISORDERS OF MATERNAL ATTACHMENT
   — CURRENT LIFE EVENTS
   A. Marital Strains
   B. Mental Illness
   C. Medical Illness
   D. Alcoholism, Drugs
   E. Financial Crises

FIGURE 1

Billy: Psychological Intervention for a Failure-to-Thrive Infant

by Selma Fraiberg

Billy was born a healthy, full-term baby, in the 70th weight percentile (eight pounds). When referred to the project five months later, he was in critical condition. Billy, now at risk, had regressed to the 25th weight percentile (14 pounds, 5 ounces), and had gained no weight in the preceding three months. The referring pediatrician described him as a failure-to-thrive baby; his mother said he vomited after each feeding.

Extensive diagnosis had revealed no medical explanation for Billy's feeding difficulties.

In her talk, Professor Fraiberg reviewed the clinical

evaluation, the emergency treatment which brought Billy to nutritional adequacy, and the home-based extended treatment which revealed and resolved the underlying conflicts between mother and child.

Bayley tests confirmed her initial impressions that Billy was above the median in motor and mental development. He was also unusually aware of sounds, and responded especially to sights and sounds related to feeding.

Despite his motor precocity, Billy rarely approached his mother, and even eye contact was lacking between this mother and child. His mother, Kathie, complained that Billy did not like to be cuddled and that when she held him, he turned away from her. Professor Fraiberg noticed, however, that Billy's parents held him facing away from them rather than embracing him in a close, ventral position. It was immediately obvious that this baby and his parents were out of synchrony. There was no spontaneity, joy, or mutual gazing in their interaction.

Billy's parents were young, had moved away from their home town, and were in great financial distress. His father, Bill, held a part-time, twelve-dollar-a-week job. Insecure as a parent, he seemed ambivalent toward Billy. During the therapist's weekly home visits, Bill would often tease, "Billy, do you want to go home with her?"

Seventeen-year-old Kathie missed her home town and friends, and regretted not having finished high school. She was overwhelmed by the sudden onset of marriage, domesticity, and motherhood. An unfinished adolescent, she had become a parent while still in need of a mother. She was extremely depressed, overweight, slow in movement, halting in speech, and suffered numerous somatic complaints (headache, backache, and gynecological problems). Both parents avoided eye contact with the therapist. This family obviously lacked the emotional and financial resources to sustain its members.

Not until their third meeting did Kathie offer to feed Billy in the therapist's presence. With the preface, "Watch what he does when I show him the bottle," Kathie set Billy's bottle on the floor. Urgently, this five-month-old crept toward his bottle, and unsteadily reached for it. After several attempts, he succeeded in grasping the bottle, his hungry mouth already open. With further struggle, he got the nipple into his mouth and sucked voraciously. Kathie complemented the scene with the rationale, "He likes it that way. He likes to have his bottle alone, on the floor."

Following this revealing scene, the therapist suggested that Kathie feed Billy in a rocking chair. Looking tired and apathetic, she held him loosely in her arms; Billy, still holding his own bottle, turned away from her. Kathie began to rock back and forth, back and forth, like a little girl rocking herself. It was more a parallel play situation than that of an adult nurturing her child.

At this point, Professor Fraiberg described the feelings of the therapist who works with infants and parents. Often, there is an urge to directly and personally rescue the endangered child, and one may feel anger toward the parents. These feelings must not be allowed to intrude, especially not in such a case as this, where the mother herself had many qualities of a child. To rescue this infant would require a thorough understanding of his child-mother's deprivation and anguish.

In subsequent home visits, the therapist expressed her strong concern for both Kathie and her baby. Kathie responded by revealing that Billy's after-meal vomiting completely unnerved her, and that she found it unbearably revolting. Following this admission, Kathie picked up Billy, who had just finished his bottle, and rushed to the bathroom. She suspended him over her arm, head down over the sink. The upside-down baby promptly vomited the contents of his meal.

Kathie further volunteered that when she had added solids to Billy's diet, the resulting hue and texture of his vomit had repelled her even more. She had responded by minimizing solid food. The time sequence coincided with Billy's weight regression.

The marginal existence of Billy's parents affected their perception of his persistent hunger. Kathie resentfully described her son as always begging for food. "If we gave him everything he wanted, he would eat us out of house and home." Bill likened his son's hunger to his own experience with hunger. "He's just like me, I could never be satisfied. I could eat everything that was given to me right now." For these parents, hunger was a part of daily living, extending to children as well.

We now had a partial picture of the parental psychopathology responsible for Billy's condition, but his condition was too critical to await the resolution of Kathie's neurosis. We decided to concentrate on the feeding problem by giving Kathie direct advice and guidance, and simultaneously, to use every opportunity to promote the attachment of baby and mother. In pursuing these objectives, we would be guided by our clinical insights into the parental psychopathology, while realizing that its full understanding would have to be deferred to a later treatment stage.

The emergency period of treatment lasted two months. The therapist soon discovered that as she responded to Kathie's needs and feelings, Kathie began to attend to Billy's needs. An acknowledgement of Kathie's distress at Billy's turning away from her was followed by renewed attempts to hold her child. Billy's nascent overtures to his mother were carefully pointed out. Kathie seized onto every bit of evidence that Billy liked her.

The first concrete change appeared in Kathie's willingness to hold Billy in her arms for a feeding, instead of giving him his bottle on the floor. When Billy continued to turn away from his mother, the therapist encouraged Kathie to tell Billy a story, and provided an example using the sing song of normal baby talk. Kathie began to recite stories to Billy and Billy quickly responded.

Kathie became able to regularly feed Billy in her arms, and we began to address her twin fears that Billy would "eat them out of house and home," and that he would invariably throw up after being fed. The therapist and Kathie established a definite, written feeding plan which gave Kathie a sense of control. Despite repeated suggestions of ways to burp Billy that would aid digestion instead of inducing vomiting, Kathie arrived at a normal burping procedure only with the therapist's active demonstration. Gradually, Kathie was persuaded to reintroduce solid foods into Billy's feeding schedule.

On a normal diet, and with the vomiting virtually ended, Billy quickly gained two and one-half pounds and moved up to the 50th weight percentile. The medical emergency was over. Psychologically, however, Billy was still very much "at risk." Now seven and a half months old, Billy still seemed to avoid eye contact with his mother. Kathie's mothering tended to be mechanical and erratic. Her ambivalence was dramatically expressed when, in the midst of an unusually successful feeding, she suddenly began to tease Billy by competing with him for his bottle. In this "harmless game," Kathie seemed to behave as a sibling.

The therapist encouraged Kathie to describe her childhood, and the pieces began to fit together. Kathie had revealed having a self-image of the unwanted middle child whom her parents felt "could never do anything right." She could barely control her rage when she spoke of her younger sister, Essie. We began to suspect that there was a ghost in Billy's nursery, and that the name of this ghost was "Essie." Essie had been the first intruder in Kathie's life, an intruder who deprived her of maternal affection and, at least in symbolic terms, of food.

If we were correct, the therapeutic goal was to get the ghost out of the nursery, to help Kathie disengage her baby from the figure of the past.

Treatment became more focused and continued for twelve months. Kathie was encouraged to talk further

about her early childhood; her pressing need to un-
burden herself made her an eager patient. We began to
move freely between the present and the past, un-
ravelling tangled memories and feelings.

Kathie remembered inventing games in which she
wreaked revenge on her intruding sister. These suggested the teasing games she played with Billy. She
recalled greatly resenting her younger sister following
her around the house, and the young child's avid gazing
at her.

Kathie's parents had forbidden her to express negative feelings toward her sister. The therapist now
acknowledged and accepted her accumulated expressions of rage and sadness. Kathie began to separate her
feelings toward Essie from her feelings toward Billy. A
pattern evolved in which Kathie's unburdening herself
of anger toward Essie enabled her to reach out to Billy,
to hold him close, and to nurture him.

As Kathie became more consistently responsive, Billy
became more spontaneous and exuberant. He turned to
her in times of joy and distress, and rapidly began to
vocalize. Professor Fraiberg and her colleagues began to
see a harmonious, synchronous relationship with many
moments of mutual delight.

DISCUSSION OF DR. BARBERO'S AND PROF.
FRAIBERG'S PAPERS. Dr. Barbero felt the central
questions of the conference were "Can you re-establish
normal mother-infant interaction and, if so, by what
kind of intervention?" Dr. Leiderman agreed that these
were the essential questions and added that models of
therapy and models of causality should be viewed
somewhat separately in order to avoid overcommitment
to any one theory of causality. He then raised the issue
of multiple attachments of the child in therapy
situations and asked Professor Fraiberg whether
Mrs. Shapiro, the therapist, had seen any evidence of
Billy becoming attached to her. She answered that she
did, to the extent of genuinely liking her and delighting
in her visits, but never by regarding her as a mother

substitute. Furthermore, the therapist avoided encouraging any such attachment, since the primary objective was to help Billy's mother develop her maternal role.

Dr. Stern pointed out that he noticed on the film shown by Professor Fraiberg that this mother did something funny while feeding the baby. She both looked at Billy and talked to him in a social manner which is a violation that no mother does unless the baby has already stopped sucking and she wants to start a play period. She probably fed him, then gazed at him. He then stopped feeding, responding to her social cues, whereupon she took the bottle away. In a sense, he is responsible for her part of the teasing also. So once again a vicious cycle occurs. Dr. Stern emphasized that in their studies, they have found that a mother will never talk to a baby while he is looking at her if the feeding is still going on, but will wait until the sucking stops.

Dr. Stern raised one of the most difficult questions of the conference when he asked if modeling (e.g., presenting the distressed mother with positive examples, as in Kathie's case) can change behavior in conflict-laden areas.

"There is no question you can help the mother by pointing out the behavioral things, but unless you can somehow shift how she feels about it, she's going to put out these cues that she's not aware of at all. Even if you can teach her. For example, 'Don't talk to the baby while you're looking at him while you're feeding him', she's going to manage somehow to give him another cue. It's really a major league question. I really don't know why a mother should be different as a therapeutic problem than any adult in any relationship."

Dr. Brazelton raised several questions about failure-to-thrive. "Why is the mother so much more of a negative stimulus and why does a baby turn so sour with failure of infant-mother interaction? Why does a certain kind of baby turn sour and others don't? When we check their previous histories, all mothers of failure-to-thrive and abused children are saying that 'this baby affected me differently'. They don't always say that the baby was defective but they say 'he affected me differently from the beginning'. They can go back to the first feeding. If you put it into the paradigm of what a mother is trying to do with her infant if she really cares, they come out with all the things Professor Fraiberg is saying about shaping and modeling. Somehow these people all care a great deal and somewhere it has gone astray."

Raven Lang described her work with postnatal groups in which midwives intentionally mother the child, and stated that this technique has been successful in teaching mothers. Ms. Arms interpreted this as providing grandmother figures.

Dr. Kennell called attention to the hospital's institutional role and its tendency to produce an unresponsive child which, in turn, affects its parents adversely. "Babies that are the miracles of modern science, the beneficiaries of superb multiple surgery, or who have spent three to four months on a respirator, are restored physically, but may have no ability to communicate with the outside world." He then described the parents' reaction as bordering on abandonment. Some of them rarely visit the child and, when they do, they pay scant attention to the child, either in a "pop-in" visit, or they spend most of the time talking with the staff.

Dr. Kennell then described his and Dr. Klaus' practice of bringing in surrogate mothers who have been "excellent with their own babies. These mothers 'fall in love' with our babies and spend up to 3-4 hours a day with them." He described the rapid response and development of the infants. Within two to four weeks they begin to have eye contact, to smile, and to respond in many other ways. This development usually elicits such a response from the infant's parents that they want to take their baby home.

Dr. Rosenblatt called attention to the infant's use of sensory systems other than the visual system. In many animal species, the infant establishes contact with its mother on another basis. Dr. Rosenblatt and his colleagues recently measured the surface temperature of a mother cat. They found that the mother cat's entire body formed a temperature gradient, with the highest temperatures at the nipple.

Dr. Rosenblatt described a succession of sensory stages in the rat, which begins with the thermal stage, then an olfactory stage, followed by a visual stage. He then referred to current research which indicates that human infants can distinguish their respective mothers by the smell of the mother's breast, and posed the question whether human mothers may vary in ability to adjust to these developmental changes in their infants. For instance, a mother may be quite capable of relating to her infant on a tactual-thermal basis, but have difficulty in adjusting to the infant when he begins to respond visually. He asked whether Professor Fraiberg had found that some mothers were capable of responding initially, but at some point could no longer respond effectively to their developing infants. It seemed to him that this would not have been the case with Billy's mother who experienced such an overwhelming aversion to primary body functions from the beginning. Professor Fraiberg replied that this was an excellent question, but that it couldn't be answered until she and her colleagues had analyzed their first hundred cases.

Dr. Barnard described the frozen watchfulness that the premature infant displays in the looking, alert state. "A normal term baby will shut you out when he's had enough. Good-bye. But the premature baby continues to stare; he can't quit until you stop. Probably for the premature infant, his mother and caretakers, vision is very important because it's one of the most available modalities through which they can interact."

Dr. Brazelton thought that "we are changing a pathological model into a positive model as we talk about it. And this is absolutely vital in terms of what you're transmitting to the parents in a therapeutic relationship. I think that everything that Dr. Barbero says about what these mothers do as they change over, which indicates a good prognosis, is, I think, identically true of a new mother and new baby; normal mother, normal baby. The kinds of things you talk about such as accepting the mothering role against all of her ambivalence, her negative ambivalence is normal. Taking on a positive distortion goes on all the time through the first month. I use it in my office inevitably to see whether a mother and father are really entering into the contract with the baby. If they say 'Oh, look, she's smiling at me', then I know she's going to make it. This kind of adultomorphic distortion is one of the most vital prognostic signs I know of in terms of observing a mother and father with a new baby."

The Relationship Between Lack of Bonding and Child Abuse and Neglect

by Ray Helfer

Dr. Helfer related the "potential" to abuse to the following five parental characteristics:

1. Neglect or abuse during the parent's early childhood which results in a missing "mothering imprint." Over 90% of the abusive parents seen by Dr. Helfer's group reported negative experiences in their own childhood.

This statistic is supported by the findings of a study recently done of approximately 100 adolescent males brought into juvenile court. When the psychologist asked how their parents handled their getting out of hand when they were small, dramatically, all but one said they were beaten.

2. Extreme personal and social isolation as exemplified by the absence of friends and supportive relationships.

Dr. Helfer described these parents as distrustful, not

liking anyone, not having any friends and not being able to relate to professionals as helpful people. Every time they went to somebody for help, someone either clobbered them, physically abused them or emotionally attacked them, saying "you're no damn good, and I'm not here to help you, so get away." The isolation of these parents is paramount. For example, of those having telephones, many more abusive than non-abusive parents questioned had unlisted numbers.

3. A poor marital relationship.

Abusive parents rarely have supporting spouse relationships, possibly because they are so poor at giving feedback. They have not learned the skills of relating to other people. Thus, the spouse they marry neither perceives nor responds to their needs.

4. Low self-esteem. The ability to think well of themselves was lost during childhood.

5. Parent-child role reversal. The parents see the child as the source of their emotional support and gratification.

When medical histories are taken and the question "what are children for?" is asked, one of three answers is heard. The mothers say, "I got pregnant so I could get out of my house" or " . . . so I would have someone to keep me company" or " . . . so I would have someone to take care of me." One mother said explicitly "sometimes I think my baby is my mother."

Add to this potential to abuse a difficult child plus any unusual stress or combination of stresses and the actual act of abuse can then occur. The precipitating event may be real or imagined, a birth defect, a social or economic disruption of the family, a difficult pregnancy or delivery, or early separation of mother and child.

Abused children have a prematurity rate twice that of the general population and a C-section rate much higher than that of the general population. The following table summarizes other findings important to the understanding of conditions related to abuse.

TABLE 1
Theories on Maternal-Infant Attachment

FACTUAL INFORMATION	ASSUMPTIONS

1.0 Early Childhood Experiences:
  1.1 85+% of abusive parents had very negative experiences as children (i.e., abused, neglected, etc.).
  1.2 60+% of physical abuse reported under the reporting law occurs in children under 6 years of age.
	1.0 Early Childhood Experiences:
	    Since the childhood was negative as far back as these parents can remember, and since most abuse occurs before the age of 6 years, then the experiences before memory (i.e., before 5 or 6 years) were also bad.

2.0 Relating to Others:
  2.1 85+% of abusive parents cannot identify one friend who could help them out in time of trouble.
  2.2 Many more abusive parents who had telephones did not have listed numbers in the directory in contrast to non-abusive parents with unlisted numbers.
	2.0 Relating to Others:
	    The development of trust and a positive self image is a learned function and abused and neglected children, as their isolation is fostered, miss out on those critical periods of development when these traits and skills are learned.

3.0 Early Separation:
  3.1 Abused children have a prematurity rate twice that of the general population.
  3.2 Abused children have a C-section rate many times that of the general population.
  3.3 Abused children are more likely to have been separated from their mothers before the age of 11 years than non-abused children.
	3.0 Early Separation:
	    Early separation of infants and somewhat older children from their mothers places the mother-baby relationship at higher risk than the general population.

The theories stated were developed from empirical and experimental observations and data in the field of child abuse and neglect.

Dr. Helfer then proposed a theory of maternal-infant attachment.

1. As a child is nurtured by his mother, the child forms a mother-baby (M-B) "memory trace."

2. The M-B "memory trace" is strengthened as interpersonal skills are developed throughout childhood.

3. The M-B "memory trace" is transmitted from generation to generation. A mother with a strong M-B "trace" will recall the memory and utilize it.

The mother with a strong "trace" can recall it despite separation from her baby of up to several months. Conversely, mothers with a weak "trace" may have difficulty in recalling the trace if separated early from their infants.

He concluded his presentation by saying that if the M-B "trace" and the behaviors which it produces (or fails to produce) could be sufficiently specified, it might be possible to recognize them in their dormant state, prior to delivery.

DISCUSSION OF DR. HELFER'S PAPER. Dr. Gardner and Professor Fraiberg questioned the adequacy of the M-B "memory trace" theory. Dr. Gardner believed the issue in question was not a 1:1 relationship between memory and experience but rather very complex inner mediating processes which arise and develop during childhood. She felt the picture to be much more complicated than that described by the M-B "trace" theory.

Professor Fraiberg believed there were better alternative explanations. She said that although nearly all her parents remember actual abuse in their childhood in stunning and chilling detail, they did not remember the affect of the experience, i.e., being abused and injured. If they were only able to help the parents reach the point of saying, "Oh, God, how I hated him when he would get that strap and lay me out and begin to beat me. Oh, how I hated him." When her group helped their parents remember the anxiety and the sense of terror that had come over them with the abuse of a powerful parent, they could demonstrate the parents' behavior toward their own children changed. Thus, she concluded, changes did not occur with just the memory of what happened, but with the actual re-experiencing of the terrifying feelings involved.

Dr. Kennell raised the question of what affects the abuse of one child had on his siblings. As a pediatrician, he has been impressed by the number of instances in which parents who abuse one of their children seem well-disposed toward the others, despite the fact that the other children appear quite abnormal, and often extremely passive.

Dr. Helfer concurred in the observation, and added his experience with the siblings of abused children who described their adaptive strategies for avoiding abuse. Passivity and over-compliance are common adaptive responses of both the abused child and his siblings. He recalled that upon hearing an abusive mother's favorable description of her childhood, he asked, "How was it with your sister when she was small?" The mother replied, "My father beat the shit right out of her."

Dr. Leiderman referred to Bayley's findings that black children are developmentally somewhat precocious, especially in psychomotor development in the first two years of life. He wondered whether this had any relation to the lower incidence of child abuse in black families in that a more active responsive child may be less likely to elicit abuse. This active versus passive child characteristic might be investigated as another variable in the etiology of abuse.

The discussion then turned to ontogeny and onset of maternal behavior. Dr. Rosenblatt reported the surprise experienced by himself and his colleagues at discovering that thirty-day-old rats exhibited maternal behavior when placed with much younger rat pups. Subsequent studies found maternal behavior as early as twenty days. "So perhaps you don't have to postulate an early 'memory trace' that is invoked later. Aspects of maternal behavior may begin to emerge very early in life."

Dr. Trause asked Dr. Stern whether, when interacting with infants, young children used the exaggerated facial expressions employed by adults with infants. Dr. Stern replied that children display maternal behavior at remarkably early ages. He described his recent pilot study in which he found animal pets elicited maternal behavior from children as young as three-and-a-half years of age. This paralleled a previously mentioned finding by Dr. Helfer that only a small number of abusive parents reported having a childhood pet, compared to non-abusive parents.

Dr. Barbero asked Dr. Rosenblatt whether there were any indications that insults during pregnancy affected maternal behavior in the rat. Dr. Rosenblatt answered that psychologically induced anxiety during pregnancy affects the emotionality of the young, but that this effect has not been established as a determinant of the subsequent maternal behavior of the young.

Returning to the subject of cross-cultural variations, Dr. Parke recommended investigating relationships between different family structures and the incidence of child abuse among American oriental, black, and Indian families as they become "Americanized." Dr. Klaus related the increase in child abuse in American black families since the 1950's to their shift from an extended family structure to the nuclear family.

Dr. Brazelton returned to the matter of infant-elicited maternal behavior. Referring to a report that stated that when people of the Kalahari desert choose which infants are to survive, they select those infants who are the best elicitors of maternal behavior, he asked Dr. Rosenblatt whether differences in maternal-eliciting qualities had been observed in rat pups. Dr. Rosenblatt explained that the pups have many qualities for eliciting response from their siblings, and that these same qualities could elicit maternal behaviors. At 18-21 days, pups will treat younger pups simply as litter mates, regardless of the latter's age (i.e., it will only huddle with it, nothing more). This is soon followed by a period during which the other pups pay little, if any, attention to the younger pups. Then suddenly, maternal behavior appears in the older pups.

Dr. Brazelton saw a parallel in the Mayan Mexican custom in which girls of only 4-6 years were allowed to nurture babies. Dr. Keefer described another human parallel behavior, the intense visual interest of 9-18 month-old infants in much younger infants, and their proximity-seeking behavior toward them.

PART TWO
THE PROCESS
OF
ATTACHMENT

The Pre- and Postpartum Regulation of Maternal Behavior in the Rat

by Jay Rosenblatt

Dr. Rosenblatt presented the thesis that different phases of the maternal behavior cycle are regulated by different types of processes. He presented evidence that the onset of maternal behavior during the rat's normal reproductive cycle is based upon hormonal secretions and that the postpartum maintenance, and probably the subsequent decline of maternal behavior, are dependent chiefly upon stimulation which the female receives from her young.

Using the hysterectomy technique which includes removal of the uterine horns, as well as the fetuses and placentas, Dr. Rosenblatt found that premature onset of maternal behavior is not confined to the period immediately preceding parturition, but that it occurs after hysterectomy at any time during the last half of pregnancy. He had earlier established that maternal behavior can be induced by continuously exposing non-pregnant females to rat pups, with a latency that averaged 5-7 days. From the 13th to the 19th day of pregnancy, latencies were significantly shortened by hysterectomy, and the speed with which females initiated maternal behavior was inversely proportional to the length of time they had been pregnant. Dr. Rosenblatt found that a large number of hysterectomized females exhibited maternal behavior within 1-2 hours, even when presented with pups for the first time, forty-eight hours after surgery. This provides strong evidence that maternal behavior is caused by endogenous changes resulting from hysterectomy, rather than being stimulated by the pups.

Subsequent experiments which included ovariectomies as well as hysterectomies resulted in significantly longer latencies, indicating that in the previous experiments, the ovaries were crucially involved in the rapid onset of maternal behavior. Dr. Rosenblatt related a particularly interesting finding of a close correlation between latencies for the onset of maternal behavior following hysterectomies performed at various times during the second half of pregnancy and the onset of the first proestrus phase of the estrus cycle. As pregnancy advances, the ovarian changes and the behavorial changes occur more rapidly.

Dr. Rosenblatt then described subsequent studies in which he attempted to restore short-latency maternal behavior in pregnant hysterectomized-ovariectomized (HO) females at various stages of pregnancy. High

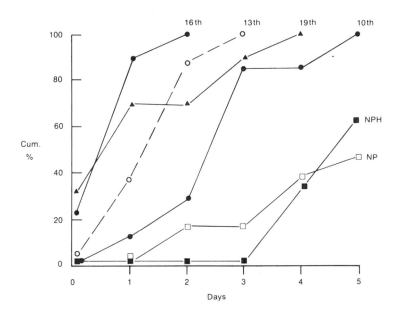

FIGURE 2

Retrieving latencies of pregnant females hysterectomized on the 10th, 13th, 16th, and 19th days and nonpregnant (NP) and nonpregnant-hysterectomized (NPH) females. Pups presented at 48 hr. postsurgery; latencies measured from beginning of pup presentation. Cumulative percentage of each group exhibiting retrieving for the first time. (Source: Rosenblatt, J. S. and Siegel, H. I. 'Hysterectomy-induced maternal behavior during pregnancy in the rat'. *Journal of Comparative and Physiological Psychology*. 89:685-700 1975.)

(25 ug) and low (5 ug) doses of estradiol benzoate (EB) were found to restore short-latency maternal behavior typical of hysterectomized pregnant females at the same stage of pregnancy. The varying latencies for the onset of maternal behavior among hysterectomized pregnant females did not appear when pregnant HO females were treated with either high or low doses of EB. Dr. Rosenblatt concluded that the progressively shorter latencies following hysterectomy during pregnancy are based upon a progressively more rapid rate of ovarian secretion of estradiol. (Figures 2, 3, 4, 5)

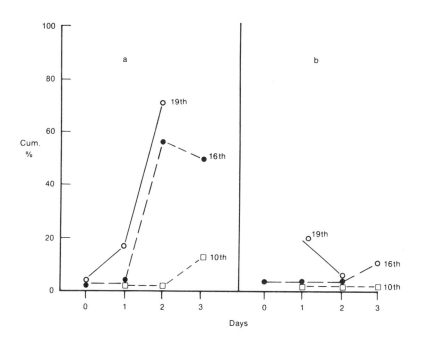

FIGURE 3

Percentage of 10-, 16-, and 19-day pregnant females of each group exhibiting retrieving in the first test after (a) hysterectomy, and (b) hysterectomy and ovariectomy following intervals of 0, 1, 2, 3 days after surgery. Each point represents a different group; N's vary from 5 to 17 females per group. (Source: Ibid.)

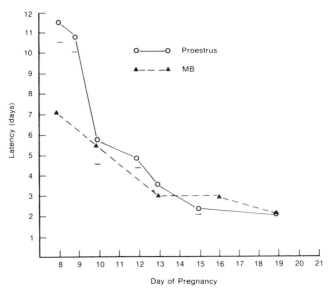

FIGURE 4

Comparison of latencies from surgery for the onset of maternal behavior and for the appearance of proestrus in females hysterectomized on the day of pregnancy shown. Median latencies for maternal (MB) and mean latencies and SE (dash below mean) for proestrus. Proestrus latencies taken from Morishige and Rothchild (1974). (Source: Ibid.)

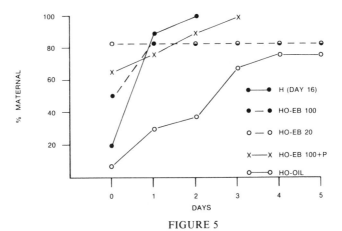

FIGURE 5

Cumulative percentage of 16-day rats becoming maternal following either hysterectomy (H) or hysterectomy-ovariectomy (HO) plus either 100 ug/kg EB and 0.5 mg progesterone (EB 100 + P), or Oil. EB injected at surgery and P at 44 hr. later. Pups presented 48 hr. postoperatively on Day 0. (Source: Siegel, H. I. and Rosenblatt, J. S. 'Hormonal basis of hysterectomy-induced maternal behavior during pregnancy in the rat'. *Hormones and Behavior.* 6:211-222 1975.)

To test whether the treatment which proved effective with pregnant HO females would also be effective with nonpregnant HO females, Dr. Rosenblatt applied the same procedure using high and low doses of EB. The high dose stimulated short-latency maternal behavior; the low dose did not. The conclusion is that nonpregnant and pregnant females differ in their sensitivity to EB induction of maternal behavior. The difference, Dr. Rosenblatt believes, may be based upon the pregnant female's prolonged exposure to gestational hormones.

Turning to postpartum regulation of maternal behavior, he presented recent evidence for its nonhormonal basis. Evidence for the nonhormonal basis had been derived from studies which showed that postpartum behavior was not affected by the absence of the pituitary glands or ovaries, nor by preventing release of prolactin, nor by injecting progesterone. "It appears, therefore, that after its onset, maternal behavior is maintained by pup stimulation acting directly upon the neural substrate of maternal behavior to maintain the female's maternal condition."

Dr. Rosenblatt described present ideas of the regulation of postpartum maternal behavior as based on studies of nonpregnant females who had been "sensitized" by prolonged exposure to young pups. Similarities in the maternal behavior of sensitized nonpregnant females and lactating mothers far outweighed the differences, and provide further support that postpartum maternal behavior is normally independent of hormone stimulation. The differences, however, are, in Dr. Rosenblatt's opinion, sufficiently significant to suggest that the mode of onset (i.e., hormonal versus sensitization) plays an important role even after the transition to nonhormonally based maternal behavior. Hormonally induced maternal behavior seems more intense, more complete, and of longer duration.

In the case of both lactating females *and* sensitized females, a period after the onset is needed during which maternal behavior is "fixed" so that it is more easily elicited at a later time. Dr. Rosenblatt suspects that some degree of adaptation to the odors of the pups is achieved in order to initiate maternal behavior but that further adaptation occurs over the first 1½ days. Once she is adapted, and can approach and remain in contact with the pups for a period of time, then other stimuli from the pups (e.g., contact, ultrasonic vocalization, suckling, etc.) which elicit maternal care can come to play an important role in regulating the female's maternal behavior.

The immediately postpartum period has been considered a "critical period" for maternal behavior and the formation of the behavioral bond between the mother and her young. Dr. Rosenblatt's studies support the conception that this period is particularly important for the later course of maternal behavior and the mother-young interaction, but his group feels that it would be wrong to conceptualize it as a "critical period." The danger is that such a formulation will encourage the isolation of developments during the "critical period" from those which precede it and those which follow. As a transition period between the hormonal onset of maternal behavior and the subsequent nonhormonal, pup-stimulated maintenance of this behavior, the immediate postpartum period is characterized by the waning of hormonal influences and the growing strength of nonhormonal influences. Many factors contribute to the outcome of the transition from pre- to postpartum regulation of maternal behavior; not all of these factors make their contribution to the outcome solely within this period. As further research gives us a better understanding of the various factors pre- and postpartum which influence the transition it will become apparent that we are dealing with a developmental sequence of interdependent phases, each of which is critical for one or another aspect of the patterns of maternal behavior.

DISCUSSION OF DR. ROSENBLATT'S PAPER.

Dr. Quilligan began the discussion by asking whether

the rat mother loses her sense of smell during the transition from prepartum to postpartum behavior. Dr. Rosenblatt replied that some investigators believed that the pregnant mother, by smelling her own body fluids, may become accustomed to the odor of her young. Dr. Kennell asked whether the prepartum and immediate postpartum self-licking was relevant. Dr. Rosenblatt answered that since the rat mother increasingly licks her genital region during the last half of pregnancy, it is possible that this familiarizes her with the odor and taste of her young.

Dr. Leiderman asked to what extent animal hormonal changes are analogous to those in the human mother, and whether the analogies are sufficient to provide a usable model. Although information on human hormonal actions is less complete, Dr. Rosenblatt explained, there are substantial analogies between the hormonal changes of the rat and the human mother, but that other animal species (i.e., the hamster) are quite different and may not provide good models. This led Dr. Leiderman to recommend a cautious approach in extrapolating from one species to another. He suggested that much more detailed information is needed.

A major difference, Dr. Rosenblatt continued, is that the rat's pregnancy is terminated by her own hormonal action, but that in the human, the mother's hormonal changes which induce parturition are initiated by hormones secreted by the fetus.

When Dr. Quilligan asked whether the hormonal changes of estrus and proestrus were essential to attachment in the rat, Dr. Rosenblatt replied that since he has been able to induce attachment in thirty-day-old pups, it seems that they do not have to experience the estrus cycle for this conditioning to take place.

Dr. Brazelton expressed a concern that the human mother must be allowed adequate time to form an attachment with her newborn. In the early transition period, she needs time for both physical recovery and for "turning inward." Expecting too much of her too soon can result in anxiety and guilt.

Dr. Rosenblatt provided the parallel that characteristically animals are exhausted by parturition and come to rest; but with animals, the resting mother offers the best position for her young to reach her nipples.

The Acquaintance Process
by Kathryn Barnard

Dr. Barnard described several studies of the early stages of the parent-infant acquaintance process. The first (Winters, 1973) was a comparison of an experimental group of mothers who were allowed to nurse their newborns while still on the delivery table. The control group first nursed their babies 4-6 hours later. All mothers in each group had initially intended to breast-feed. Two months after delivery, 5 of the 6 "delivery table" mothers (i.e., the experimental group) were still breast-feeding compared with one mother in the control group.

The mothers in the control group who were no longer breast-feeding had stopped within approximately two weeks. These mothers said that the baby did not suck well and it was not a satisfying experience for them. Conversely, "There was an overwhelming response from the mothers in the experimental group to describe the experience of the early months and particularly the breast-feeding as very satisfying and positive," Dr. Barnard said.

The second study (Ryan, 1973) involved a "Mother Brazelton," an adaptation of the neonatal exam developed by T. Berry Brazelton. The "Mother Brazelton" was designed to show the mother the unique characteristics of her baby. Mothers in both control and experimental groups were given a letter at the time of delivery explaining some of the items on the Brazelton exam, both at the reflexive and orientation levels. Two days following the delivery, the investigators demonstrated the "Mother Brazelton" to the experimental mothers with their own babies. The mothers' perceptions of their babies were measured at two days and again at one month of age with the Broussard scale. At these same times, the baby's behavior was also measured, independent of the mother demonstration. Although Dr. Barnard's team did not find a significant difference in terms of either the baby's behavior or in the mother's perception of her baby, they did note that the experimental mothers had a more positive attitude toward their babies than the control group. The experimental mothers reported fewer sleeping problems and fewer feeding problems.

Intrigued by this apparent trend, Dr. Barnard and her colleagues (Kang, 1974) repeated the study altering several of the variables. In this study the modified Brazelton was demonstrated to both the mothers and fathers in the experimental group by a nurse during a home visit when the baby was two weeks old. Dr. Barnard found that at that time the "parents were primed for a demonstration of their baby's unique behavior in terms of looking, hearing, orienting, crying, and being consoled."

When both groups of babies were measured at one week of age using the Brazelton assessment, no difference in alertness was found. However, when the babies were tested again at one month of age, the experimental babies were significantly more alert. As measured by the Broussard scale, the experimental mothers and fathers were significantly more positive in their attitudes toward their babies than the control parents, consistently describing them as "better than average children."

Lastly, Dr. Barnard described a study of the sleep-wake activity of the premature infant (Barnard, 1974). The experimental infants who were between 33 and 34 weeks gestational age were placed in a special rocking bed which was equipped with a recording of a human heart beat. The rocking bed and heart were programmed to automatically turn on every hour for fifteen minutes in an effort to provide repetitive low frequency stimuli. Dr. Barnard studied the effect of the heart beat and rocking on the sleep-wake activity patterns of the infants. She found that by the second week of the program, the amount of quiet sleep had increased. The experimental group gained more weight than the control group who were not on the rocking heart program and had Dubowitz scores that indicated an increased maturational level.

A follow-up study, to examine the possible long-term effects of the stimulation, was conducted about a year and a half later. The babies in the experimental group had Bayley Mental and Motor Scores 10 to 12 points higher than the control babies. All of the experimental babies were above the 10th percentile in height while only half of the babies in the control group were above the 10th percentile. The Caldwell Home Stimulation Inventory indicated that the pattern of maternal stimulation was higher in the experimental group than in the control group.

According to Dr. Barnard, the results of this study convinced her "of the ability the infant has to turn on mothering behavior in the mother."

DISCUSSION OF DR. BARNARD'S PAPER. In the discussion following Dr. Barnard's talk, Professor Fraiberg suggested that "it might have been interesting, if in the control group, too, there had been a visit from the nurse without any discussion of the Brazelton to see what happens in view of the fact that we have seen some changes that we know have not yet been the result of our inventions but simply from the first or second home visit."

Dr. Brazelton asked Dr. Barnard to discuss the two ways she assesses mother-infant interaction. Dr. Barnard explained that they had developed two scales. "One is to look at the mother-infant interaction during feeding situations and the other is to look at mother-infant interaction during a teaching situation. Things we ask her to teach are age level items on the Bayley, and one that's about a month and a half advanced. On the feeding scale, we're trying to look at mothers' behaviors and behaviors that are interactive. For instance, one of the interactive behaviors was control. Who has control of the situation? Who decides what's going to happen next? Some of the maternal behaviors that we look at are focus. What is the mother's focus during feeding? Is it on interaction? Is it on getting food in? We look at her position of the infant and the two things we record are how she is positioned in regards to the safety and comfort of the infant and how is the position in relation to interaction? Is it supporting or facilitating interaction or not? We look at the amount of kinesthetic stimulation. How much auditory? How much visual? We have two verbals: Verbal I is the complexity of the verbalizations with the child and the other, Verbal II the contingency of her verbalizations. We also observe two response times: response time I relates to how she responds to distress in the infant. Does it take very powerful distress cues, like crying or thrashing around before she responds or does she respond to subtle ones? And response time II is how does she respond to signs of satiation. It's interesting, you'll find mothers who can respond beautifully to distress but absolutely block out any cue about the child being satiated."

Evidence for a Sensitive Period in the Human Mother

by John Kennell

Dr. Kennell explained that although the large number of complex factors that influence maternal behavior in the human make it difficult to determine whether there is a sensitive or special attachment period immediately after delivery, the possible effects could be so far reaching that there is a compelling need for careful investigation. He then proceeded to review the scientific studies relevant to the question of a sensitive period and their implications, and raised questions for further study.

Studies of animal behavior have provided many striking examples of a critical and time-limited maternal sensitive period. In a variety of species, separation during the first few hours, or even minutes, after delivery results in the mother rejecting or neglecting her young when they are reunited.

An attachment can be defined as a unique emotional relationship between two individuals which is specific and endures through time. The maternal sensitive period is conceptualized as that time, following delivery, in which the mother forms, or begins to form, an attachment to her infant. It is hypothesized that "during this sensitive period, a cascade of reciprocal interactions begins between mother and infant which locks them together and mediates further attachment. This is the optimal, although not the sole period for an attachment to develop."

Dramatic evidence of a sensitive period in the human mother has been provided in instances where mothers have inadvertently been given the wrong baby. Dr. Kennell described such an incident which occurred in an Israeli hospital. In this and in similar incidents, the mothers had become so attached to the "wrong" baby that they hesitated to give it up later, even for their own biological baby. He then related personal clinical experience with mothers who were separated from their infants during the newborn period, e.g., with premature and high-risk infants. He described these mothers as being noticeably more hesitant and clumsy in learning basic mothering tasks such as feeding and diapering. Mothers of these infants sometimes momentarily forgot they even had a baby, and often reported that they felt the baby really belonged to the head nurse or the physician.

As further evidence of the effects of separation on the development of attachment, Dr. Kennell cited the much higher incidence of child abuse and failure-to-thrive without organic cause among premature infants.

He reported that even the brief separation caused by mild neonatal illnesses, such as a mild elevation of serum bilirubin levels or transient tachypnea, appear to affect the relationship between mother and infant. Even where the infant's problems have been resolved within a few hours, Dr. Kennell has observed the mother's behavior to be disturbed throughout the first year and longer.

Continuing, Dr. Kennell described a number of studies which varied in the time of initial mother-neonate contact and then measured the outcome. He first described a carefully controlled study in which the experimental group of mothers were given early and extended contact with their babies for one hour beginning one to two hours after delivery and for five hours on each of the three succeeding days. Compared to the control group which received care which is routine in U.S. hospitals (a glimpse of the baby at birth, followed by 20-30 minute feeding visits every 4 hours), mothers in the experimental group showed significantly different maternal behavior. At one month, they were observed to maintain greater proximity to their infants, to show much more soothing behavior during a physical examination of the infant and to engage in more eye-to-eye contact and fondling of their infants during a filmed feeding. At one year, similar behavioral differences persisted. At two years, these early-contact mothers were observed to exhibit distinctive linguistic behaviors with their children. They used fewer commands, asked twice as many questions in talking to their children, and used more adjectives and fewer content words.

Dr. Kennell cited other studies where the maternal

MOTHERS OF FULL TERM INFANTS

STUDY	NUMBER	HOUR OF FIRST CONTACT	DEPENDENT VARIABLES	RESULTS
KLAUS, et al.	28	1 vs. 12	ATTACHMENT BEHAVIOR 1 and 12 MONTHS SPEECH AT 24 MONTHS	EARLY>LATE **
KENNELL, KLAUS, MATA, SOSA and URRUTIA	19	1 vs. 12	ATTACHMENT BEHAVIOR AT 12 HOURS	EARLY>LATE**

** p<.05 (Non-Parametric)

FIGURE 6

behavior of early-contact mothers was compared with mothers who had only the contact provided by prevailing hospital practice. (Figures 6, 7, 8) In every study except one, in which the baby was allowed contact with the mother's nipple, early-contact mothers were more successful in breast-feeding, and in one investigation the

MOTHERS OF FULL TERM INFANTS

STUDY	NUMBER	HOUR OF FIRST CONTACT	DEPENDENT VARIABLES	RESULTS
WINTERS KENNELL, KLAUS, MATA SOSA, URRUTIA	12	1 vs. 16	BREASTFEEDING AT 2 MONTHS	EARLY 6/6 LATE 1/6**
A) IGSS HOSPITAL	38	1 vs. 12	WEIGHT GAIN IN 35 DAYS	EARLY 1186 gms. LATE 1010 gms.*
B) HOSPITAL ROOSEVELT	62	1 vs. 12	WEIGHT GAIN IN 35 DAYS	EARLY 934 gms. LATE 928 gms.
SOUSA	200	1 vs. 12	BREASTFEEDING AT 2 MONTHS	EARLY 77% LATE 27%*

*p<.05 (t test)
**p<.05 (Non-Parametric)

FIGURE 7

mean weight of the early-contact infants at 35 days was 6 ounces greater than that of the controls.

In conclusion, Dr. Kennell cited a study at Case Western Reserve University in which one group of mothers was allowed to enter the nursery and touch their premature babies in the first week and another group was permitted tactile contact after 21 days. When tested at 42 months, children in the early-contact group attained significantly higher Stanford-Binet scores. The mean I.Q. was 99 vs. 85 for those who were first touched by their mothers after three weeks. A significant corre-

MOTHERS OF PREMATURE INFANTS

STUDY	DAY OF FIRST CONTACT	DEPENDENT VARIABLE	RESULTS
LEIFER, LEIDERMAN, BARNETT and WILLIAMS	1-5 vs. 21	ATTACHMENT BEHAVIOR	SIGNIFICANT INTERACTIONS OF SEX AND PARITY
		DIVORCES	LATE 5 vs. 1
		RELINQUISHED THE BABY	LATE 2 vs. 0
KENNELL, KLAUS	1-5 vs. 21	EYES ON BABY AT DISCHARGE FEEDING	EARLY>LATE*
		I.Q. at 42 MOS.	EARLY 99 vs. 85*

*p<.05 (ANOVA)

FIGURE 8

lation was also found between the I.Q. score at 42 months and the amount of time the mothers looked at their babies during feedings, which had been filmed at the time of discharge from the nursery. Since mothers with early contact looked at their babies more at the time of the one-month feeding, these findings indicate that early contact affects aspects of mothering behavior which may have significance for the child's later development.

DISCUSSION OF DR. KENNELL'S PAPER. Dr. Helfer asked Dr. Kennell whether the mothers who were allowed to visit their infants in the nursery considered themselves as special people with special privileges. Dr. Kennell explained that the visiting and non-visiting practice alternated on a monthly basis during the study, so that at any one time, either all mothers were allowed in the nursery, or all were excluded. To Dr. Brazelton's inquiry of whether the mothers who were allowed to visit have "lived up to" the researcher's implicit expectations, Dr. Kennell replied that every effort was made to treat control and experimental groups identically, e.g., each group received the same amount of time and attention.

Dr. Rosenblatt questioned whether maternal behavior is inherently directed toward a specific infant, and asked Dr. Kennell whether he supported this view versus the possibility that maternal behavior becomes specific with time and experience. Although the data are insufficient and inconclusive, Dr. Kennell has been impressed by the tendency of mothers who had been separated from their infants to spend hours going from one infant's bed to another when visiting their own child in the hospital. This contrasts sharply with the early-contact mother of a hospitalized infant who tends to spend all of her visiting time with her own infant.

Dr. Rosenblatt, referring to a study of goat maternal behavior cited earlier by Dr. Kennell, stressed the observation that if the goat was allowed to lick her newborn for only the first minute or two, the mother would accept all young, but when allowed to lick for five minutes, she would accept only her own young. Dr. Rosenblatt interpreted this as proof that the brief licking established maternal behavior, and that prolonged licking made the behavior specific. He further pointed out that animals vary regarding the specific quality of their maternal behavior. It tends to be very specific in species where the young must be protected; where protection is unimportant, or unnecessary, the mother may never even know her young.

Summarizing his clinical experiences with mothers who had been given the wrong baby, Dr. Brazelton said that he had found them to be devastatingly upset by apparently "being able to nurse any baby." Their attitude seems to be, "My job is to get to know *this* baby." He is convinced that attachment occurs very early in labor and delivery, and that there is a specificity which is very important to the mother. A mother once told him that to think she could nurse "any" baby made it more difficult to separate her real baby from the one she dreamed about during pregnancy.

Dr. Klaus observed that mothers who had been given the wrong baby have great difficulty in relinquishing them. Even when the error had persisted for only fifteen minutes, they had great difficulty in transferring their full affection to their own restored infant — often reminiscing, "that was such a lovely baby."

Dr. Trause expressed general agreement with

Dr. Rosenblatt's view that maternal behavior was not necessarily specifically oriented to one particular infant, whereas, she said, attachment by definition was. One cannot be attached to people in general, but only to particular individuals. Although maternal behavior and attachment behavior are "intertwined" in the human, maternal or caregiving behavior cannot always be considered an indication that a specific attachment exists. For example, one can feed a baby without being attached to it.

Professor Fraiberg commented that although she did not want to overdo the visual aspects, she and her colleagues have observed that both in the mothers who have blind-from-birth infants and in the researchers who did not share the personal tragedy, there was a difference in response to the babies who did not make eye contact. There was a disturbance in the initial attachment or relationship to the baby. Because the sign system was so alien to both the mothers and the researchers (the sign system of need, of affection, of exchange), it took a considerable time for the researchers or parents to understand what the baby was communicating. The help the researchers offered the parents was an important part of the bonding process. She ended by comparing the process to falling in love which is also not understood very well.

Dr. Stern showed the timelessness of these questions by quoting Dante, "How long does the fire of love in a woman endure when the eyes and touch are no longer there to kindle it?"

Ms. Arms expressed exasperation with the general reluctance to accept the importance and benefits of early mother-infant contact. Dr. Klaus agreed that obstetricians had not accepted it, and Dr. Quilligan added that pediatricians have, in fact, enhanced separation, " . . . the first thing the pediatrician does is to put the baby in an isolette and get it out of the delivery room."

Returning to the subjects of attachment and specificity, Dr. Rosamund Gardner described a physiological and experimental basis for specific maternal attachment. "The mother has a certain amount of specificity enrolled because she has carried the child for nine months — an overwhelming reason why she should feel particularly attached to that child since it has been attached to her body for nine months. There's an enormous carry-over from the physiological feelings of the mother during the pregnancy to the actual realization of this piece of herself that is now 'out there'. These are bodily experiences which are very close to the somatic levels of love, and I don't think there's any mystery about that — except in the male mind."

Delivery in the Home
by Raven Lang

After showing a film of a highly successful home delivery, Ms. Raven Lang described her role as supportive, encouraging the parents to make their own decisions, rather than "dictatorial." As an example, her mothers make their own choice of the position in which they wish to deliver. They often defer making this choice until the actual time of delivery. Ms. Lang cited statistics that in a group of 289 women, 39% elected to give birth on their hands and knees. She teaches the fathers to massage the mother's perineum during delivery, a method which she has found very effective in avoiding perineal tearing and the need for episiotomies.

Both Ms. Lang and Ms. Nancy Mills, a midwife active in Sonoma County, have found many of their home deliveries form a communal event. The expectant parents sometimes invite as many as 10 or 12 close friends and relatives to attend the delivery. Some of those attending write descriptions of the event and collect such descriptions of other communal home deliveries. "The child is, and continues to be, special

to those who participated in its birth." Ms. Mills
added that the mothers rarely experienced postpartum
depression.

Dr. Klaus asked whether this communal participa-
tion in the past was a fail-safe device which provided
alternative caretakers similar to those provided by the
extended family in cultures with high maternal mortality. The participants in the delivery do, in fact, serve
as caregivers when the mother has difficulty in nurturing
the child.

Returning to the statistical observations, Ms. Lang
added that in a study of 289 women who elected home
delivery, 231 delivered with no complications, 13 delivered (at home) with slight complications, 45 delivered
in the hospital, 7 had cesarean sections, and one baby
was stillborn. She compared the extrapolated perinatal
mortality for this group, 3.2 per 1000, to the U.S.
national average of 27.1. Furthermore, she added, all
except 10 of these mothers gave birth without either
analgesia or anesthesia, and the average Apgar score for
the babies was 9.14 at 1 minute, and 9.17 at 5 minutes.
The prematurity rate was 2.2% compared with the
national average of 6.7%. Dr. Brazelton added that he
had heard of a midwife program in rural Alabama,
which, within two years, reduced fetal mortality from
28/1000 to 7½ per 1000.

Ms. Lang expressed strong conviction that the more
favorable statistics were the result of the home delivery's
more natural environment and the childbirth education
which the midwives provided in their prenatal care. She
spends approximately 30 hours with each expectant
mother prior to delivery, usually with the older siblings
present, and frequently with the husband in attendance.
The clinic with which Ms. Mills is affiliated provides a
course in husband-coached childbirth. In their prenatal
home visits, Ms. Lang and Ms. Mills emphasize prenatal
care including nutrition, discuss the mother's needs,
goals, and expectations, and advise her on how to
conduct herself during labor and delivery. After the

delivery, they provide follow-up visits according to the mother's needs, usually daily visits for the first 3 or 4 days following birth and then at one or two week intervals.

Elaborating on the advantages of the home delivery program, she referred to research findings that show fear reduces uterine blood flow and decreases the amount of oxygen available to the fetus. Regarding the environmental influence, she cited Dr. Niles Newton's experiments with mice in "artificial environments similar to a hospital"; she related that labor was 72% longer and that the pup mortality was 54% higher than for the control mice in normal settings. With the apparent implication that delivery position was a factor, Ms. Lang referred to recent research at Stanford which indicates that the supine delivery position results in fetal hypoxia. She questioned the need for routine episiotomy since only 6.6% of women were torn when delivered by experienced midwives.

Dr. Helfer commented that the health statistics cited earlier for the home deliveries could be the result of the parents' unique childbirth preparation, or that this group of mothers was healthier than the general population. Further research is necessary to separate the two variables. In a similar vein, Dr. Brazelton stated that prenatal care is a major issue in reducing mortality, and that these home delivery mothers were a highly select group regarding prenatal care. Ms. Mills agreed, calling attention to the inherently greater continuity of care provided by the midwife in contrast to hospital care.

In responding to the very blunt question, "Is home delivery really necessary?", Ms. Lang presented her reasons for favoring home delivery under present circumstances, and her ideal of a maternity setting. She explained that psychologically, hospitals are places of sickness and disease and in her opinion inherently inappropriate for birth. The physical, visual and social characteristics of the hospital institution appear alien to the needs and expectations of many mothers. Consequently, many mothers elect home delivery not expressly for its own sake, but as the only alternative to the hospital. As an alternative, Ms. Lang described her "utopian" design for a maternal setting. It would completely avoid the institutional look of a hospital, all the necessary hospital apparatus would be immediately available, but out of view in an adjacent area. Delivery would take place on a low bed, close to the floor. The design would be one in which the mother dictates her own behavior and controls the birth. The facility would be amenable to accommodating the husband, as well as siblings, relatives, and friends.

At Dr. Kennell's invitation, and as the consultant obstetrician at this meeting, Dr. Quilligan provided the following comments:

"It is difficult to argue with the success shown in your films, and we certainly do many things in hospitals which I personally regard as barbaric. Barbaric traditions can be broken. However, since it is very difficult to predict which mothers and which babies are going to have difficulty in labor, I think the most feasible alternative lies in your suggestion that an environment be created for that 97% of normal deliveries, with adjacent facilities for the 3% of problem deliveries. This would permit doing a cesarean section in 3 minutes rather than in the 30 minutes that it would take to get from the home to the hospital and set up the operation. That time saved will mean far fewer brain damaged babies. England had home deliveries for a long time, complete with their 'flying squads' — mobile units which took care of home deliveries where problems developed. They ran into enough trouble to decide to abandon the practice."

Ms. Mills questioned whether the reversal of home deliveries in England was more likely due to "Americanization." Ms. Arms described Holland as providing a strong case for home delivery. "Holland encourages home births, and in Holland, approximately 50% of deliveries take place in the home." In contrast to

England, she has found that Dutch midwives neither provide nor encourage mothers to use analgesics or anesthetics.

Ms. Mills added that she and her midwife colleagues explain to their expectant mothers the nature and risks of home births, and advise them that, as midwives, they do not offer anesthesia.

Asked to comment on anesthesia, episiotomy, and delivery position, Dr. Quilligan agreed that in many instances the lithotomy position is awkward and uncomfortable. He explained that it had become standard with obstetricians because of its advantages in difficult deliveries. "I believe a straight-forward, spontaneous delivery should be performed in any position that the mother finds comfortable." Although he agreed that the supine position caused some decrease in uterine blood flow, he strongly disagreed with the earlier statement that the supine position causes fetal hypoxia.

Dr. Rosenblatt suggested that the evolutionary aspect should be investigated, citing evidence that evolution has produced strong mechanisms which favor certain delivery positions, and that institutionally imposed routines may be violating these mechanisms. There is strong evidence that in lower animals, birth postures have a hormonal determinant, which suggests that when the human mother is restrained, she is being restrained against the action of hormones. "There are natural movements — if only she would be allowed to make them." Dr. Rosenblatt continued by describing recent work being conducted in his laboratory on sexual reflexes in the rat. They discovered that if one stimulates the cervix in the rat as it is normally stimulated during sexual relations, the female is immediately inhibited in her response to all tactile stimulation. There is a direct inhibition of all painful stimulation of a tactile sort. Thus, it appears that through evolution, nature has provided a mechanism to compensate for the fact that the birth process may be painful. Dr. Rosenblatt concluded his comment by cautioning that some of our practices may actually violate the mechanisms that have evolved as beneficial.

Dr. Quilligan then addressed the subject of episiotomies, and explained that they had become routine because women had a great deal of relaxation following multiple spontaneous deliveries. "The parity rate is significantly lower now, and we certainly know more about how to control delivery. A well-conducted study might reveal that there is no longer sufficient need for routine episiotomies; at present, we simply don't have the answer."

Dr. Quilligan began his comment on anesthesia with the statement, "Obviously, medication is a poison." But he hastened to urge a comprehensive view of the issue. In a difficult and excessively uncomfortable labor, the mother may secrete large amounts of epinephrine and norepinephrine which can reduce uterine blood flow and decrease the baby's oxygen. In such cases, he explained, mild amounts of analgesia, which relieve the pain, anxiety, and tension, may benefit the baby by mitigating the mother's physiologic responses. Recounting his experience with childbirth education as a practicing obstetrician, Dr. Quilligan described it as an effective method, but only for the highly motivated, not for the "general population."

Ms. Mills countered this qualified endorsement by describing her success in coaching mothers through difficult deliveries, without anesthesia. The thrust-and-parry of this discussion did not end there. Dr. Quilligan responded that as a result of personal acquaintance with Dr. Grantly Dick-Read, he knew that some mothers whom Dr. Read delivered vowed never again to repeat the experience, because "Dr. Read mesmerized them into something which they didn't want to go through ... You can't overcome a culture in 30 hours or even in nine months. You can't overcome what might have gone on in childhood, the way the mother has influenced this particular girl about what childbirth is all about. She may have made it so negative that you cannot make it positive."

Having acquitted himself of this paradox, Dr. Quilligan was then invited by Dr. Klaus to resolve another dilemma. Dr. Klaus described the prevailing U.S. hospital delivery as one in which the physician is in total control: "He decides where and when the delivery takes place, with stirrups or without, and who is allowed or not allowed to be present." He contrasted this with Ms. Lang's home deliveries in which the mother controls these matters, and raised the question whether mother-infant attachment might be favored by the latter situation where the mother is an active participant rather than being "acted upon." Dr. Klaus then asked Dr. Quilligan, "How can we get the best of both worlds? The advantages of modern obstetrics and perinatology, and have the mother as an active participant?"

Dr. Quilligan replied that a viable solution was offered in Ms. Lang's proposal for a maternal setting in close proximity to a hospital, possibly he added, within the hospital. Ms. Lang reiterated her conviction that it should not be in the hospital itself. Dr. Brazelton drew attention to the implications of such radical changes for medical education, citing the need to "change the whole orientation of medical students and doctors from a pathology-oriented approach to delivery and taking care of babies."

Ms. Arms saw a continuing need for mothers to maintain the initiative, "Mothers are going to have to refuse things that are demanded of them at the time when they are most vulnerable. They'll have to say, 'I don't want to be supine', or 'Don't give me glucose'." She concluded by pointing out the difficulty of maintaining such a role when the doctor says, "It's for the baby's good." Dr. Quilligan countered, "And many times it is."

Professor Fraiberg drew attention to the unique relationship between the midwife and her home delivery parents. An unusually strong bond is formed between

them, and the amount of time devoted to each preparation (30 hours for Ms. Lang) was well beyond the
capability of most obstetricians and clinics.

Mother-Infant Reciprocity
by T. Berry Brazelton

Dr. Brazelton described his goal as the development
of a method for assessing the affective communication
system which develops between infants and their caregivers within the first few months of life. Such a method
would make it possible to understand the necessary
ingredients for optimal infant-caregiver interaction.
With such understanding, it may be possible to measure
the caregiver's sensitivity to the infant, and to identify
failure(s) in communication.

In analyzing mother-infant interactions in the first
four months of life, Dr. Brazelton has used a split screen
technique to videotape simultaneously the interacting
normal mother and her alert infant. The videotape
includes a time indicator which makes possible the
analysis of mother-infant behaviors in fine detail.

Through these observations, he has found that even at
two to three weeks, the infant has two clearly distin-
guishable "sets" of behaviors and attention-nonattention
cycles for interacting with people in contrast to objects.
Interaction with objects involves a short and intense
exploration appropriate for obtaining the limited
amount of information from objects. This contrasts with
the neonate's more cyclical pattern of attention for
prolonged investment in social situations where he
learns cognitive and affective information from his
caregiver.

While interacting with a person, all parts of the
infant's body move in cyclical patterns, outward to the
person (attention) then back towards his body (nonattention). This ebb and flow of attention occurs several

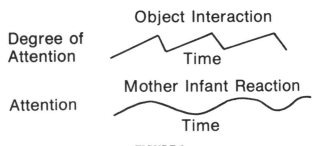

FIGURE 9

Alternating attention and nonattention with object and mother. (Source: Brazelton, T. B., Koslowski, B. and Main, M., "The origins of reciprocity: the early mother-infant interaction," in Lewis, M. and Rosenblum, L., Eds., *The Effect of the Infant on its Caregiver,* New York: John Wiley and Sons, 1974.)

times per minute. Without such an economical homeostatic model, he might easily be overwhelmed by the many cues flowing from another human in a short period of time.

As the infant who is interacting with a person approaches the peak of his attention cycle, he slowly reaches out and coos, his eyes dilate and both arms jerk forward, his head moves backward, and his face brightens. He then appears to reach a limit and begins to turn away. This begins the cycle of nonattention in which the infant seems to recover or readjust. His eyes shift from his mother's face to a point beyond her and his hand grasps his shirt, "place-holding" as he overtly tries to maintain this nonattention despite her continuing cues. Several seconds later, he slowly returns his gaze toward his mother, lets go of his shirt and smiles faintly as he begins a new attention cycle. When in synchrony, his mother increases her behaviors (in frequency and in intensity) as he approaches the peak of his attention cycle, then decreases her behaviors as he shifts to nonattention. These attention and nonattention behaviors form a behavioral curve which resembles the homeostatic curves which dominate all of the infant physiologic systems.

Mother and infant seem to become synchronous with

each other in these cycles which include the following phases:

1. Initiation,
2. Orientation, which establishes the partner's expectations regarding interaction,
3. Acceleration to a peak of excitement,
4. Deceleration, and
5. Turning away.

The partners have a good interaction when they synchronize both their attention-nonattention cycles *and* the individual phases of their cycles. An infant who is constantly bombarded by an insensitive mother will quickly establish a pattern of prolonged nonattention and brief periods of attention.

To determine how early an infant develops an expectancy for interaction, and to delineate some of the interaction's ingredients, Dr. Ed Tronich in Dr. Brazelton's group decided to interfere with face-to-face interaction at three weeks. After a period of normal interaction, he asked mothers to maintain a still face for three minutes. After a brief attempt at interaction the infant becomes aware that his normal expectancy is not being fulfilled. He responds with brief attempts to elicit a response, followed by "waiting" periods. The extent and urgency of the attempt to elicit response is especially impressive. After repeated failures to get his mother back on track, however, he withdraws and seems to expect no response. It is striking that in failure-to-thrive infants, the withdrawal is seen in the extreme as a wariness and aversion.

When caregivers learn a failure-to-thrive's rhythms and overcome his wariness by repeated rewarding contact, the infant begins to interact and become responsive. This often takes two weeks. Dr. Daniel Rosenn has designed a scale which can predict the weight gain in a failure-to-thrive infant by scaling his responsiveness to caregivers. Within a day or so after this responsiveness is established, the failure-to-thrive

first starts to gain weight. To develop the psychophysiological mechanisms for gaining weight, the infant must
first be served with rewarding emotional experiences.

Dr. Brazelton explained that the infant's homeostatic
cyclical curve of attention allows him to modulate the
sensory stimulation available to him. He can shut out
excessive information which might overwhelm him.
Synchronous rhythms between infant and mother (or
other primary caregiver) are essential for his development. If we can better define the essential interaction
and help the mother or çaregiver to shape her patterns
to the infant, we may be able to bring about a therapeutic attachment. Dr. Brazelton hopes to explore the
use of videotape for giving parents greater insight into
their infant's rhythmic availability.

He cited Dr. Barnard's work with brain-damaged
children as a major contribution as a precedent.
Mothers are understandably repelled by the disturbing
movements of these children. The therapist learns to
synchronize her movements with the infant. As the baby
picks up this information from the therapist and shows
how rewarded he feels, the mother is inspired to imitate
the therapist and, for the first time, becomes
synchronous with her damaged infant.

Failure to meet the infant's need for synchrony violates the rules for interaction, rules which are vital not
only to his development but for his very survival.

Through these experiences, Dr. Brazelton and his
fellow investigators soon became aware that there was
an immense variety of maternal behavior clusters which
stimulated the infant, and that the mother-infant interaction could not be described by a simple stimulus-
response model. Only a cyclical model of attention
could explain the infant's ability to "pick up" on diverse
and shifting combinations of stimuli. The cyclical
pattern of attention and recovery enables him to mon-
itor the input of information from the other member of
the dyad. By regulating the duration of his cycles, he is
able to handle the unpredictability of his partner and to

adjust to disturbing interactions. This cyclical pattern must be at the center of the infant's ability to maintain a balance in the face of the physiologic demands on an immature regulatory system.

If a mother is insensitive to the cyclical pattern of her infant, she may overload his capacity for prolonged attention. Dr. Brazelton has found that infants respond to overloading by establishing prolonged nonattention and brief periods of attention. The pattern can emerge by the infant's sixth week and may provide a sign for early detection of pathology.

He has been especially impressed by the infant's "hunger or drive" to elicit and maintain face-to-face interaction and with the seriousness of his withdrawal when his efforts fail. In failure-to-thrive infants, this eagerness has been replaced by wariness and aversion, similar to the normal infant's behavior when his mother violates his expectancy for response. As the disturbed infant's wariness is overcome by repeated rewarding contact with caregivers (especially when they learn his rhythms), the non-thriving infant develops a greediness which allows him to go from one person to another without fear. In a therapeutic setting with an opportunity for meaningful interaction, a deepening attachment to one or a few caregivers occurs soon thereafter. Within a day or so of this deeper attachment, the infant rapidly gains weight. This physiologic counterpart of the affective mode emphasizes the fact that the infant must receive rewarding emotional experiences if he is to develop the psychophysiological means for thriving.

The homeostatic cyclical curve of attention allows the infant to prolong his attention to an expanding world of mother, then father, then other adults who are sensitive to his needs and rules. It also provides him with a rich matrix for decision-making. He can modulate input, and can shape his curve to meet the demands of his dyadic partners.

The rhythmicity between primary caregiver and infant is an essential ingredient in their developing relationship. Dr. Brazelton is convinced that, in a "good" interaction, mother and baby synchronize from the beginning. Pathways may be established even during intrauterine life to be entrained by the mother immediately after birth. "Intrauterine experience with other maternal cues, such as auditory and kinesthetic cues, may well set the stage for enhancing the meaning of the synchronous rhythms. We are pretty sure that a mother who is sensitive to her infant's needs can enhance his capacity to attend to her important cues within a few weeks."

Conversely, he warned that, "without this kind of attention to a baby's needs for synchrony and facial expression, we may well expect not just a failure in communication and static lack of development, but a real violation of complex, expected and necessary rules for interaction which are basic to survival, and without them, withdrawal from social interaction and regression of development and physiologic progress."

Infant and Mother at Play
by Daniel Stern

Dr. Stern described his work as similar to Dr. Brazelton's in that both study interaction between the mother and her baby and both use videotape split screen techniques to analyze minute details of behavior. The major difference in their methods is that the Brazelton studies are conducted in a laboratory setting whereas Dr. Stern's group goes into the home. Dr. Stern, however, pointed out that he has not found that mother's behavior changes very much from one setting to the other.

In order to begin to understand the rules of human interaction, Dr. Stern said he began to study play situations between mother and baby, since play is so purely social. He focused on gaze as an initial variable because of the extraordinary fact that by three to four months of age, the baby has essentially a functionally mature visual-motor system. This means the baby can stop looking whenever it pleases by turning away or closing its eyes. Thus, when you watch a mother and baby look at each other, what you are watching is two people who have essentially equal control over the same behavior in their interaction. Dr. Stern believes this is the only kind of behavior in such young infants that functions both as a perceptual and motor system for social purposes.

From a purely experimental viewpoint, gazing behavior is useful to study because it can be described by mathematical models which include just four states:

1. Mother and infant can both look at each other,
2. Mother can look away while baby continues looking,
3. Baby can look away while mother continues looking, or
4. Both can look away.

By analyzing what each partner did every .6 seconds of their interaction, Dr. Stern calculated the probability of one's state (e.g., both looking at each other) staying the same or changing into one of the other three. For example, if neither mother nor infant is looking at the other at one interval in time, they will continue to not look at each other during the next .6 second interval (with a probability of .60). To get out of this state, the most likely change is that the mother will look at the infant.

Dr. Stern found that the baby's attention repeatedly cycles toward and away from the mother. Thus, most of the action was back and forth between mutual gaze, baby's breaking gaze while mother continues holding gaze, then baby's looking back. As Dr. Brazelton reported, both are attuned to react to each other so that no matter what happens, they spend an immense amount of time moving towards mutual gaze position.

Dr. Stern believes that observing mother-infant interaction in terms of these units helps determine when
something is wrong. For example, some mothers will
put the baby down, thus stopping the interaction. Other
mothers will not let the baby look away; they'll move
and follow its gaze. Dr. Stern finds the latter an easy
way to diagnose a controlling mother.

After many of these observations, Dr. Stern and his
colleagues were struck by what the mother did to hold
the infant's gaze and attention. Mothers do extraordinary maneuvers with their voices and facial movements
when they are with their babies. He has come to call
these behaviors "infant-elicited variations of normal
behavior." The most obvious example is baby talk
which Ferguson has found to be a universal human
phenomenon. In addition, both mothers and fathers will
speak in a falsetto range and use extreme variations in
pitch and stress which give a sing-song quality to their
voices. Vowel duration is elongated to give "oohs" and
"aahs."

Mothers also use extremely unusual facial expressions while talking to their infants. They greatly
exaggerate and slow down the movement of their
eyebrows and mouths while attempting to hold their
infant's attention. The most common expression is
similar to greeting behavior which Dr. Stern calls "the
mock surprise expression." The essential ingredients are
raising the eyebrows, throwing the head back and
opening the mouth, often saying "ooh" or "aah." This,
according to Dr. Stern, is the payoff or high point of the
interaction.

Mothers also do goofy things with their gaze to hold
the baby's attention. They lock in mutual gaze with their
babies for 15 to 30 seconds at a time which nobody else
does in this society, unless they are either going to fight
or make love. Mothers also violate norms of interpersonal distance by moving very close to their infants,
often wagging or cocking their heads in unusual ways.
Thus, the baby is exposed to extraordinary ranges of

human behavior.

Dr. Stern has recently moved to the study of a larger unit of interaction behavior which he calls "games." A game is a repetitive set of behaviors done over and over again with only slight variations by the mother or father over a short period of time. A simple one is peek-a-boo which the mother will do four or five times the same way. Then she may add "aah" or kiss the baby's belly or move back in mock surprise, then kiss the belly again.

The intriguing question to Dr. Stern is how the baby cues the mother to change the game. He finds that one important signal is the infant's response decrement in gazing which indicates his waning interest. Also, the infant's facial expressions suggest his state and whether mother must vary her strategy to keep his attention.

Although there are too many possible games to catalogue them all, Dr. Stern has found there are some that seem to be stereotypes. One of these he calls "punch line behavior" because mother and baby get together and start revving each other up. The baby gets excited, moving its head and the mother smiles back and they keep going back and forth until the game reaches a climax. Both peel off in excitement similar to when a joke has finished, then after a pause, return to interaction at a lower level of arousal.

Dr. Stern concluded by speculating about the function of play and the game. He suggested that because babies become bored easily, mothers who are interested in holding their infant's attention must create new ways to capture them. Thus, the system is always in flux and drives both mother and infant into new transformations of behavior, both joyful and aggressive. This constantly expands the nature of the interaction so that in a sensitive, well-working system, the baby is exposed to a great variety of stimulation. Essentially, the infant becomes more experienced about what it is like to be involved in human interaction and the variety and richness of the stimulation becomes enormous.

From a practical viewpoint, Dr. Stern felt that

mothers who do not provide stimulating games can be taught to do so easily, thus increasing the potential rewards of the interaction for both mother and infant.

DISCUSSION OF PAPER BY DRS. BRAZELTON AND STERN. Professor Fraiberg began the discussion by commenting that Dr. Stern's game material happens to have very rich clinical applications, giving more information than feeding situations, for example, in the assessment of interactions between mothers and their blind infants. She said she could almost read the attachment profile from the game profile, since the parent who is in trouble is the parent who violates the game.

Dr. Helfer agreed that the abusive parents who are his patients also have trouble in these areas; they have difficulty creating games to engage their infants. His special problem, however, involves the dilemma of whether to remove a particular child from the home for the sake of his own safety. He finds that the children respond more quickly than the parents in the learning and training situations. If the children are kept in the home, they are penalized because their development is slowed to that of the mother. However, if the child is removed from the home, the mother is penalized because she does not have a child with whom to relate to learn these skills. An added risk, he pointed out, especially in child abuse, is that if the child is stimulated by other people to do things that the mother cannot tolerate, like acting like a child, he is in more danger of being injured.

Dr. Brazelton answered this by suggesting the adoption of the model developed by Drs. Klaus and Kennell in their work with mothers of premature infants. These mothers have been presented with a nurturing environment which expected them to do well in a situation known to be particularly stressful. He emphasized that usually in hospital environments nobody expects people to behave differently than in the past, so their negative behaviors are reinforced. His group has used items from the Brazelton scale to show mothers what their potentially brain damaged infants could do. Then they set goals within the limits of the babies' capacities and rhythms. Within two weeks, the mothers had made unbelievable strides because their expectations for working with their babies had been changed. "By changing our medical attitudes," he concluded, "we can do a hell of a lot . . . Let's change our pathological eyes into some normative eyes and I think then the parents can keep up with the children as they progress. We must have the interaction as our focus, rather than just the child."

Dr. Rosenblatt introduced another line of discussion by speculating about what makes infants respond to stimulation. He began by explaining that every sensory system has a search pattern. Kittens have a search pattern that involves side-to-side movements of the head in order to find the nipple of a mother who is lying down. Goats move their heads up and down because the mother is standing. What Drs. Brazelton and Stern have described among human infants is a periodic pattern of visually searching the environment. What catches their interest, Dr. Rosenblatt believes, can be understood through Schneirla's work which shows that the early basis of responding for newborns is the physical characteristics of stimulation rather than its meaning. These include such factors as the intensity of the stimulus which is produced by the rate of movement, the amount of contrast and the amount of space covered by the movement. There is an optimal range of stimulation which attracts the infant; below this is too weak to be arousing, whereas above is too strong and will elicit withdrawal. Dr. Rosenblatt suggested that parents intuitively find that optimal range and stay within it. They keep varying the stimulation within the range, however, so the infant does not lose interest. Parental behaviors like raising the eyebrows and lowering the head constitute changes in the physical characteristics of the stimulus.

Dr. Stern agreed that he was using Schneirla's model of an optimal range of arousal or stimulation. The baby is always peripherally monitoring the mother. If she does not provide enough stimulation, the baby does not center his attention on her. If she provides too much, on the other hand, the baby will turn away. Dr. Stern added that the interaction is a two-way street. If there is something wrong with the baby so that it cannot put its stimulation into the system, then the infant-elicited maternal behaviors will not appear. As a result, the stimulation within the system remains low because the baby is not a good elicitor.

Dr. Brazelton further elaborated that infants are capable of performing well-organized behaviors in the first days of life. He cited MacFarlane's findings that three-day-old babies reliably turn toward their mother's, rather than a strange woman's breast pads when one is placed on each side of his head. The infant can do this while the mother is still producing colostrum before she is actually lactating.

Dr. Leiderman refocused the discussion by stressing the need to specify clearly the ages and cultural backgrounds of babies being described. He said he wished to underscore the tremendous variation among infants and families and the resistance to change of some early formed cultural components. He illustrated the range of differences in practice by describing the caretaking arrangements in a village where he worked in Africa. There, the infant was traditionally carried around and cared for by its 7- or 8-year-old sister, with the mother supervising. One could not, however, generalize about infants in other settings from this particular arrangement.

Dr. Stern picked up this thread by contrasting how highly aroused babies from Western industrialized societies are in comparison to those from a more primitive society like the Kalahari desert. In the latter setting, as soon as the baby stirs, the mother brings it to breast and gives it a couple sips of milk. The baby is fed every thirty minutes, so he never has to build up to a high arousal level where he's crying because he's hungry. Secondly, if the baby moves, the mother knows because it is lying right next to her. In the West, the baby is usually in another room or certainly in another bed, and the only way to communicate with the sleeping mother is by crying, by reaching a high level of arousal. In other words, to yell or scream. Similarly in play interactions, Western mothers, particularly middle class ones, are good at keeping the baby at an upper level of excitement. "Perhaps," Dr. Stern concluded, "this is why we are such a keyed up bunch of people."

Ms. Lang brought the discussion to a close by commenting that over and over again she has noticed pregnant women stroking their stomachs. They usually rub the lower portion of the uterus, back and forth, and sometimes with two hands. She suggested that this rhythm is the beginning of communication and is perhaps something that could be measured. Dr. Barnard added that it seemed to her that when anything is important in human behavior there are practice periods before it is necessary.

Father-Infant Interaction

by Ross D. Parke

Dr. Parke described hospital practices which exclude the father from early interaction with his infant as reflecting and reinforcing a cultural stereotype. Both our culture and the theories guiding our research have focused on the maternal role in early infancy, largely ignoring the father. The very lack of research on father-infant interaction has further reinforced the assumption that fathers are uninterested in young infants and are unimportant at that stage. However, recent modifications in hospital practices and the renewed interest in home deliveries indicate a changing view of the father's role. Dr. Parke speculated that some of the motives instigating home deliveries may be the father's desire to have a more active role.

Dr. Parke first assigned himself the task of investigating to what extent fathers interact with their 2- to 4-day-old infants in a hospital situation. He conducted his first study in Madison, Wisconsin with a small, middle class group of parents of 9 male and 10 female infants. Half of the group had attended childbirth education classes and with one exception, the fathers attended both labor and delivery. Except for one cesarean section, all deliveries were spontaneous; 13 of the 20 infants in the study were breast-fed, the remaining 7 were bottle-fed.

Parents were observed in two different situations: the mother, alone with the infant at 2-4 days of age, and father, mother, and infant together in the mother's hospital room (i.e., triadic interaction). In a second study, observations of the father alone with the infant were included.

Observation included a sampling procedure in which investigators recorded the occurrence or non-occurrence of infant and parent behaviors in each of forty 15-second intervals for 10 consecutive minutes. The selected infant behaviors consisted of:

Crying	Looking at father
Vocalizing	Looking at mother
Moving	Looking around

Selected parent behaviors consisted of:

Looking at infant	Touching infant
Smiling at infant	Imitating infant
Vocalizing to infant	Exploring infant
Holding infant	Feeding infant
Kissing infant	Handing infant to other parent

The advantage of studying individual parent behavior as well as triadic interaction, Dr. Parke explained, is that the latter demonstrated what Bronfenbrenner describes as second-order effects. These are defined as the impact of the presence of a third person on the pattern of interaction of two individuals. In these studies, Dr. Parke asked what effect the mother had on the interaction of the father and infant and vice versa.

The initial study revealed that, in the triadic situation, the father tends to hold the baby nearly twice as much as the mother, vocalizes more, touches the baby slightly more, and smiles at the baby significantly less than the mother. The father clearly plays the more active role when both parents are present, in contrast to the cultural stereotype of the father as a passive participant. In fact, in this triadic interaction the mother's overall interaction declined.

Dr. Parke described the initial study as limited by the small number of middle class participants, half of whom had taken a course in childbirth education; and, all but one of the fathers had attended labor and delivery. Each of these factors could be expected to produce an unusual degree of father-infant interaction. He conducted a subsequent study using the same design and techniques at a large metropolitan general hospital in Cincinnati with lower income families and a much higher incidence of premature and high risk infants. Childbirth education is a rarity in this setting and fathers are not allowed in labor and delivery rooms. Despite these social and institutional differences, the Cincinnati study revealed the same pattern; in the triadic interaction, the fathers clearly played the more active and dominant role. They held the infant more than the mothers did, vocalized more, and touched more. As in the Madison study, the mothers smiled at the baby more often than did the fathers. The principal difference in the Cincinnati study was that the father, rather than the mother, tended to take responsibility for the feeding.

Further analysis revealed that the father's presence significantly influenced the mother's affect. In the father's presence, mothers smiled more often at their infant and explored more.

"The father-mother component of triadic interaction was not investigated and must be included," said Dr. Parke, "in order to obtain a complete triadic analysis." To date, Dr. Parke's studies have not revealed any significant behavioral differences between fathers alone with their infants and mothers alone with their infants. He interprets this as clear evidence of parallels between maternal and paternal behavior, but not as proof that differences do not exist. "We used an axe to attack a delicate and subtle problem" was his way of describing the initial investigations, and he explained the need for more discriminating methods in future investigations. One hypothesis to be explored is that mothers are more "caretaking-oriented" (e.g., more concerned with feeding, diapering, and consoling their infants), while fathers are more "play-oriented" (e.g., more concerned with playful, stimulating interactions with their infants).

Additional variables which warrant careful analysis were identified by Dr. Parke as the sex and ordinal position (birth order) of the infant, medication of the mother, anesthetics and analgesia, and infant social responsivity (e.g., as measured by the Brazelton Scale). He described his preliminary findings that fathers appear more responsive to first-born boys and that mothers spend more time stimulating their high medication infants (but father interaction showed a negative correlation with the medication variable). He has also observed positive correlations between infant social responsivity (as measured by the Brazelton Scale) and mother-infant interaction. For fathers, the correlation tends to be lower and is negative for some Brazelton measures — such as irritability. "It's almost as if the father is a much more delicate organism." The infant must be relatively active and responsive to capture his attention.

In a tentative conclusion, Dr. Parke reviewed his findings as indicating that the father is much more involved in and responsive toward his infant than our culture has acknowledged. (Follow-up studies are in progress to determine whether hospital observations of early parent-infant interaction can serve to predict later interaction.) The initial findings regarding father-infant interaction and the triadic interaction hold wide implications ranging from the social-cultural level to hospital practice. A critical issue for Dr. Parke is that the care of infants be acknowledged as natural and appropriate male behavior. If the father-infant role and the father's role in triadic interaction is to be fully realized, Dr. Parke is convinced that the father must have extensive early exposure to the infant in the hospital where the parent-infant bond is initially formed. "There is a lot of learning that goes on between the mother and infant in the hospital — from which the father is excluded, and in which he must be included so he'll not only have the interest and a feeling of owning the baby, but also the kinds of skills that the mother develops." In closing, he referred to Margaret Mead's observation that fathers are a biological necessity, but a social accident, and charged his audience with the task of "bringing the father back into the family from the start and demonstrating that he is a social as well as a biological necessity."

PART THREE
PROBLEMS
OF
ATTACHMENT

Innovations in the Premature Nursery: A Survey of Parental Visiting and Related Practice

by Rose Grobstein

Ms. Grobstein presented the findings of a study which she and Drs. Barnett and Seashore began in 1970 to investigate parental visiting and related practices in U.S. premature nurseries.

Questionnaires were mailed to the 2,729 premature nurseries listed by the American Hospital Association. This yielded a return of 61% (1,644 nurseries responding); 1,444 of the returned questionnaires provided usable information, thus representing a 52% sample of the target population. The sample over-represented Western hospitals and underrepresented Southern hospitals. The proportion of North-Eastern and North-Central hospitals conformed to their distributions in the AHA list.

Thirty-four percent (486) of the responding nurseries had adopted the practice of allowing mothers to visit and to handle their infants in the premature nursery. Of these nurseries, 60% also allowed the father free entry. Investigation of the sequence of related innovations found that the adoption of parental visiting was usually preceded by relaxation of aseptic precautions and by encouraging increased handling of infants (for stimulation) by house staff.

Surprisingly, premature nurseries with medical school affiliations were not the pioneers of parent visiting and related innovations. By 1964, 15% of premature nurseries allowed mothers to have contact with their infants. Nurseries which had instituted this and related innovations by 1965 were classified as early adopters. Nurseries affiliated with medical schools had not instituted innovations significantly earlier than non-affiliated nurseries. By late 1970, however, medical school affiliated nurseries had adopted significantly more of these innovations than had their non-affiliated counterparts.

In this study, Ms. Grobstein and her colleagues investigated the information sources used by nurseries in reaching policy decisions on parent visiting. They found that those which instituted parent visiting at an earlier date relied heavily upon their experience with mothers of premature infants, this source being cited by over one-third of the early adopters. The following is a typical account:

> In May of 1965, we had a three-month-old baby, who had been with us for three months, expire from a heart condition. At no time had we considered the feelings of the parents who had visited every single day, standing at the observation window. When the baby died, the mother asked to hold him. Crying, she rocked him and explained this was the first time she had ever touched him. From that time on, all mothers of prematures are allowed to scrub and gown and to touch their baby in the incubator, regardless of the baby's condition.

Nurseries which adopted the practice at later dates reported more formal information sources. Thirty-five percent reported first learning of parent visitation practices at workshops in other local hospitals, 25% from a visiting physician or nurse, and 22% while attending national pediatric or nursing meetings.

The relative unimportance of reading as a source of information presented a second surprise to Ms. Grobstein and her colleagues. Of the small group that mentioned reading as a source, 20% cited either *The Reader's Digest,* various women's magazines, or a local newspaper. This led the investigators to question the organization and effectiveness of communication concerning pediatric innovations. They also called attention to the tendency of many nurseries to perpetuate practices long abandoned by the American Academy of Pediatrics newborn care manual (e.g., masks for regular nursery personnel) while ignoring recommended practices such as gowning.

Of the 486 nurseries which offered parent visiting, only 8 (1.6%) reported having based their decision on research (either bacteriological or psychological). Eighty-one percent cited "common sense" as their reason for allowing mothers into the nursery. Ms. Grobstein made several objections to this rationale. The fact that only a minority (34%) of the responding nurseries allow mothers into the nursery conflicts with such a justification. In earlier years, she continued, an intuitive approach may have been more acceptable, but there has since emerged sufficient research on infant development and mother-infant interaction to allow a more scientific approach to nursery care. She emphasized that the purpose of this study was not to encourage the innovations surveyed, but to qualify them and to investigate their etiology. In conclusion, Ms. Grobstein stressed the need for a more scientific approach to nursery care which assigns high priority to the psychological and social needs of parents and infants. "If the social organization of nursery care ignores these," she warned, "the trend will continue toward avoidance of professional, institutional care — as evidenced by the increase in home births and similar 'natural' practices which defeat the application of modern obstetrics and pediatrics."

Mother-Infant Separation: Delayed Consequences

by Herb Leiderman

Dr. Leiderman summarized the salient findings of earlier mother-premature-infant research at Stanford University. The type and amount of social interaction in the immediate postpartum period, including its interruption (separation) was found to significantly affect maternal and infant behavior as well as the mother's attitude toward herself and her baby. "Separation of a mother from her premature infant for as short a time as 3 weeks in the immediate postpartum period can lead to lowered feelings of maternal competency and decreased maternal attachment, sometimes continuing for as long as 1 month following their reunion."

He then turned to the data from the analysis of a two-year follow-up study. These findings fit into three categories:

1. Maternal attitude, based on interview with the mother,
2. Maternal behavior, based on observations of the mother in a caretaking role,
3. Infant behavior, based on the infant's scores on a standardized test.

The outstanding finding was that separation of mother and infant during the prematurity period has little influence on either maternal behavior and attitude 12 months after separation or infant performance 15 months after discharge. The only effect found for separation was that mothers who had not been separated touched their infants more than separated mothers, regardless of the infant's birth order or sex. A more complex finding was that mothers of non-separated male infants and mothers of separated female infants laughed with, and smiled and talked to their infants more than mothers in other corresponding groups.

The most significant finding was the relationship between maternal behavior and infant performance and the infant's birth order and sex. Primiparous mothers are higher than multiparous mothers on almost any behavior observed. They spent much more time with their infants in non-specific play and distal attachment behaviors including looking, talking, smiling, and laughing. Sex of the infant, however, primarily affected proximal attachment behaviors including touch and holding. Mothers of male infants touched their infants more, whereas mothers of female infants spent greater amounts of time holding their infants.

Dr. Leiderman made a distinction between two principal types of factors which affect the mother-infant relationship and its development. These are temporal determinants and structural determinants. Temporal determinants include the time of initiation, continuity, and quality of maternal contact with the newborn. Structural determinants refer to the sex and birth order of the infants and possibly an array of socioeconomic variables. He finished by emphasizing that we cannot just take the temporal effects into consideration in attempting to understand the mother's relationship to her infant. The structural factors such as social class, sex, and birth order may play an even greater role in determining how particular women behave as mothers.

DISCUSSION OF PAPERS BY DR. PARKE, MS. GROBSTEIN AND DR. LEIDERMAN. Dr. Barbero asked whether any relationship had been found between husband-participation in labor and delivery and the incidence of divorce. Ms. Lang replied that she had observed a relationship between difficult labor and infant deaths and subsequent divorce, and conversely, that "the easy, lovely, and wonderful labors seem to have the opposite effect; they seem to give the father a new insight into the strength and courage of his wife, and he becomes more supportive." Dr. Leiderman had recently reviewed divorce statistics for one of his experimental groups and replied that five of the seven divorces occurred in families where mother and infant both had been separated, but low economic status appeared to play an equal, if not greater, role. He described the process as one of multiple stresses, "low economic status plus prematurity plus separation."

Dr. Brazelton further emphasized the role of economic conditions by reporting on a recent paper by Cravieto and Chavez that was presented at the nutrition conferences in Atlantic City. The researchers found that by providing mothers with food supplements throughout pregnancy and the first year of their infants' lives, the behavior of the children was radically affected. They talked in longer sentences, used adjectives, and did not give commands. The babies were much more active and moved away from their mothers more. The fathers got locked into the system compared to the families splitting up in the control group. Dr. Brazelton was impressed with the wide-spread effects of the intervention.

Regarding birth order, Ms. Lang reported observing instances of stronger attachment between parents and their second-born infant in cases where the first-born had been delivered in the hospital and separated from the mother and the second-born had been delivered at home where no separation occurred. Dr. Rosenblatt cautioned that the preferential treatment given the first-born could have adverse effects, especially when the preference includes excessive expectations of his performance. The issue was carried further by Dr. Helfer's comment: "I don't think we know, in the long run, whether more holding, touching, and smiling is good or bad." As an example, he related that in observing non-human primates, when a mother spends an abnormal amount of time feeding her infant, the question arises whether this represents superior stimulation or simply inefficient mothering. Dr. Trause had observed behavioral differences between one-year-old first-borns and later borns when separated from mothers in the presence of strangers. Her first impression was that first-borns were less upset by situation, but then she considered the alternative hypothesis that first-borns expressed their distress in a more socially acceptable manner (i.e., by becoming very quiet or withdrawn instead of yelling and screaming).

The discussion then moved to the role of fathers in child abuse. Dr. Helfer explained that although 90% of mothers reported they were married when the abused child was born, most of them were in some way separated from that relationship at the time of abuse.

This does not necessarily mean that the mother does the abusing, but merely that she is living singly. There may be a man present, but rarely is he doing anything with the children. Furthermore, if the man is not married to the woman with whom he is living, he is in a unique legal position because he has no responsibilities. If the case of abuse goes to court, he cannot be involved with that proceeding in any way unless criminal charges are brought. This, Dr. Helfer stated, would be extremely unusual. Thus, the unmarried man is not legally responsible for anything that happens with that child.

Dr. Helfer continued saying that the social system fosters fatherless arrangements. The woman who has a baby and keeps it can get assistance whether the father stays around or not. Dr. Helfer concluded by reporting that abusive mothers are likely not to use birth control or have an abortion so that they are likely to have a higher birth rate than non-abusive mothers.

Dr. Rosenblatt commented that among animals, abuse by a father only occurs when he is not the biological father. For example, it has been reported among monkeys that when one male takes over as the dominant male, he will kill all the young of the former male. He does that, suggests Dr. Rosenblatt, to bring the female into reproductive readiness which does not occur while she is lactating. This fits a newly emerging theory that there is a mechanism whereby organisms protect their own genetic material. Many predictions can be made on that basis.

Dr. Klaus reported some important data of Dr. John Lind, which demonstrate that when the fathers were asked to undress their babies twice and establish eye-to-eye contact with them in the first days of life, they showed significantly more caregiving behavior than did controls three months later. Dr. Parke agreed that his data show that it is possible to get fathers involved. The remaining question then is what kind of structural social support is needed to produce and maintain those changes in paternal behavior.

Dr. Klaus changed the discussion by asking Ms. Grobstein how to manage the mother's profound concerns when her sick newborn infant is transported to a large intensive care center while she remains behind. He told of a movement that is being studied which proposed bringing the high risk expectant mother to a high risk center before her baby is born so she can deliver it near adequate intensive care facilities.

Ms. Grobstein replied that with the use of resources and planning in the proper way, we should be able to bring the high risk mothers that have been identified to an intensive care center for delivery or to bring them both together to the center after the birth of the baby. Adequate living facilities for them and possibly for their families would have to be provided. But, she thought the expense would not be greater than the kind of medical care currently being delivered.

Dr. Brazelton concluded the discussion by emphasizing the importance of keeping the mother involved when necessity demands that her baby be transported away from her. The nurses in his unit send a picture to the mother and call her every day in the hospital. They tell her what the baby is like, not just the condition, not what his temperature is, but what he looks like, what he behaves like. When the nurses make a big effort to say "the baby needs you," the mother gets there as soon as she is out of the hospital and the chance to bond later is tremendously increased.

Closing Comments

Dr. Kennell suggested that a few minutes of open-ended commentaries might be the most appropriate ending for the conference.

Dr. Rosenblatt contrasted the "state of the art" in the late 1940's (when there was still considerable question whether experience played a role in early development) to the enormous amount of recent and contemporary research in the field.

Dr. Klaus saw as a major challenge, the task of combining the qualities shown in Ms. Lang's home deliveries with the advances in modern hospital obstetrics and pediatrics. The implications of current knowledge about parent-infant interaction are sufficient to require reorientation not only in hospital care, but in medical education as well.

For Professor Fraiberg, the meeting had dramatized "the abyss between what we know and what we can bring into practice." She had one reservation, that the excitement and synthesis of experience flowing from the meeting might wither unless some continuity was formalized, hopefully in the form of regular meetings. Paralleling Ms. Grobstein's concern for a more rational basis for policy and decision making, Professor Fraiberg called for a program of post-doctoral fellowships which would expand access to the type of information exchanged at this meeting, information which is rarely available in a single hospital or university.

The vote for a continuing dialogue was seconded by Dr. Helfer who found special value in the meeting's broad coverage of the normal and the pathological. Dr. Gardner found an equally important integration of therapy and basic research. She described the meeting as a format which momentarily freed the therapists from their clinics and the researchers from their laboratories, and which provided group communication, exchange of theories and innovation, complete with "the clash of personalities. It's a rich setting to get your mind going, and I thank everyone for it."

Dr. Kennell paid tribute to the contributions of Raven Lang and Nancy Mills, midwives devoted to the needs of infants and parents, for "bringing us a great truth which we have often missed along the way, the innate truth of our fellow men."

References

Barnard, K. E. The effects of stimulation on the sleep behavior of the premature infant. *Communicating Nursing Research.* (Ed.) Batey, M. Wiche, 1974.

Barnard, K. E. and Douglas, H. B. Child Health Assessment, Part I: A Review of the Literature, U.S. Government Printing Office, DHEW, HRA, Division of Nursing, Publication No. (HRA) 75-30, pp. 1-211.

Barnett, C. R., Leiderman, P. H., Grobstein, R. and Klaus, M. Neonatal separation: the maternal side of interactional deprivation. *Pediatrics* 54:197-205, 1970.

Brazelton, T. B. Neonatal behavioral assessment scale. *Clinics in Developmental Medicine.* Number 50. Philadelphia: J. B. Lippincott Co., 1974.

Brazelton, T. B., Koslowski, B. and Main, M. Origins of reciprocity. In M. Lewis and L. Rosenblum (Eds.) *Origins of Behavior,* Vol. 1, New York: John Wiley & Sons, 1973.

Broussard, E. and Hartner, M. Maternal perception of the neonate as related to development. *Child Psychology and Human Development* 1(1):16-25, 1970.

Fraiberg, S. Blind infants and their mothers: an examination of the sign system. In M. Lewis and L. Rosenblum (Eds.) *Origins of Behavior,* Vol. 1, New York: John Wiley & Sons, 1973.

Fraiberg, S., Adelson, E. and Shapiro, V. Ghosts in the nursery: a psychoanalytic approach to the problems of impaired infant-mother relationships. *J. Amer. Acad. Child Psychiatry,* 1975.

Helfer, R. and Kempe, C. (Eds.). *The Battered Child.* University of Chicago Press, Chicago, 1968.

Kennell, J. H. and Klaus, M. H. Care of the mother of the high-risk infant. *Clinical Obstetrics and Gynecology* 14:926-954, 1971.

Klaus, M., Jerauld, K., Kreger, N., McAlpine, W., Steffa, M. and Kennell, J. Maternal attachment — importance of the first postpartum days. *New England Journal of Medicine* 286:460-463, 1972.

Lang, R. *Birth Book,* Genesis Press, 1972.

Leiderman, P., Leifer, A., Seashore, M., Barnett, C. and Grobstein, R. Mother-infant interaction: effects of early deprivation, prior experience and sex of infant. *Early Development* 51, 1973.

Leifer, A., Leiderman, P., Barnett, C., and Williams, J. Effects of mother-infant separation on maternal attachment behavior. *Child Development* 43:1203-1218, 1972.

Parke, R. Family interaction in the newborn period: some findings, some observations, and some unresolved issues. In K. Riegel and J. Meacham (Eds.), *Proceedings of the International Society for Study of Behavior Development,* 1974.

Parke, R. D., O'Leary S. and West, S. Mother-father-newborn interaction: effects of maternal medication, labor, and sex of infant. *American Psychological Association Proceedings,* 1972, 85-86.

Quilligan, E. J. and Paul, R. H. Fetal monitoring: Is it worth it? *Obstetrics and Gynecology* 45:96, 1975.

Rosenblatt, J. The pre- and postpartum regulation of maternal behavior in the rat. *The Parent-Infant Relationship.* Ciba Foundation, 1975.

Stern, D. A micro-analysis of mother-infant interaction. *Journal of American Academy of Child Psychiatry* 10:3, 1971.

Stern, D. Mother and infant at play: the dyadic inter-action involving facial, vocal and gaze behaviors. In M. Lewis and L. Rosenblum (Eds.) *Origins of Behavior,* Vol. 1, New York: John Wiley & Sons, 1973.

Terkel, J. and Rosenblatt, J. Humoral factors under-lying maternal behavior at parturition: cross-trans-fusion between freely moving rats. *Journal of Comparative and Physiological Psychology* 80:365-371, 1972.